OLD MOORE'S

HOROSCOPE
AND ASTRAL
DIARY

•

LEO

foulsham
LONDON • NEW YORK • TORONTO • SYDNEY

foulsham
Yeovil Road, Slough, Berkshire, SL1 4JH

ISBN 0-572-02007-4

Printed in: Great Britain at
Cox & Wyman Ltd, Reading

CONTENTS

OLD MOORE'S HOROSCOPE AND ASTRAL DIARY

Old Moore's Horoscope and Astral Diary represents a major departure from the usual format of publications dedicated to popular Sun-sign astrology. In this book, more attention than ever before has been focused on the discovery of the 'real you', through a wealth of astrological information, presented in an easy to follow and interesting form, and designed to provide a comprehensive insight into your fundamental nature.

The interplay of the Sun and Moon form complex cycles that are brought to bear on each of us in different ways. In the pages that follow I will explain how a knowledge of these patterns in your life can make relationships with others easier and general success more possible. Realising when your mind and body are at their most active or inactive, and at what times your greatest efforts are liable to see you winning through, can be of tremendous importance. In addition, your interaction with other zodiac types is explored, together with a comprehensive explanation of your Sun-sign nature.

In the Astral Diary you will discover a day to day reading covering a fifteen month period. The readings are compiled from solar, lunar and planetary relationships as they bear upon your own zodiac sign. In addition, easy to follow graphic charts offer you at a glance an understanding of the way that your personal life-cycles are running; what days are best for maximum effort and when your system is likely to be regenerating.

Because some people want to look deeper into the fascinating world of personal astrology, there is a section of the book allowing a more in-depth appraisal of the all important zodiac sign that was 'Rising' at the time of your birth and another showing what bearing your 'Descending' sign has on relationships. Beyond this you can learn about the very real part that the Moon has to play in your life.,

From a simple to follow diary section, on to an intimate understanding of the ever changing child of the solar system that you are, my Horoscope and Astral Diary will allow you to unlock potential that you never even suspected you had.

With the help and guidance of the following pages, Old Moore wishes you a happy and prosperous future.

HERE'S LOOKING AT YOU

A ZODIAC PORTRAIT OF LEO
(23rd JULY - 23rd AUGUST).

The most usual description of Leo emphasises a fine crop of hair, often in the form of abundant curls and sometimes looking like the Lion's mane itself. Added to this, the general bearing is regal and fine, with the head held high and proud. Generally speaking these facts are a good reflection of what lies beneath the mantle, for in this sign we find strength in abundance and a sunny disposition that is almost majestic at its best. Most Leos have power and vitality, even in a physical sense; endurance to keep going when others fail, yet at the same time the apparent laziness that is indicative of all cats.

In matters of dress and general appearance, Leo people have a love of adornment, though the Lion is an instinctive follower, rather than a leader of, fashion. All the same, the image is all important because all cats have to preen themselves to perfection and the chances are that you are no exception to the rule. In conversation the Leo is frank, free and often outspoken, Perhaps the greatest virtue, when viewed by the world as a whole, is generosity, both in a material sense and with regard to intellectual matters too. A conscientious streak makes you keen to fulfil your responsibilities to the full and in relationships you are ardent, sincere and quite passionate.

The best position for you to be in is one that puts you at the forefront of affairs; well, you do represent the King of the jungle after all! On the other hand you make a very poor follower and are miserable if you cannot take the most important part in the moulding of your own destiny. Fortune usually attends your endeavours, despite the fact that you can sometimes lose out as a result of being too ambitious and exhibiting a determination to do things in your own way, even when a little help would go a long way. What you do show in abundance is optimism, together with the kind of help and support that the rest of the world can find to be invaluable. At the end of the day these may turn out to be the most important qualities.

THE INTENTION

Leos are natural actors, even the quiet ones. They were born into this world already in possession of dramatic showmanship, a quality that is displayed at any and every opportunity. So often it is the impression made that matters even more than the situation itself. This need for show can lead to personal extravagance on the part of the Leo, and let's face it, the Lion is as generous with him/herself as he/she is with the rest of the world. People warm to Leos, most just can't help doing so; for despite a certain naive quality the Lion has tremendous generosity of spirit, a force that can bring out the best in others too. The Leo ego would be large enough for three people of almost any other sign, and yet a natural affability and honour makes this seem somehow unimportant.

Deep inside, the essence of the Leo nature is a need to be 'special', to come to terms with one's own identity and uniqueness. Leo seeks to find the creative spark that lies within, the essence of 'being', which is why so many Leo people become artists of one sort or another. Strong Leonine types need to offer their many skills to the world at large in order to be fulfilled completely, yet another reflection of the ego that lies within and part of the self-love that is so important to this sign.

If the desire to show themselves off to the world as they really are is thwarted, the Leo nature can take a deviation away from the frank cheerfulness that everyone loves and cherishes, displaying itself ultimately as self-aggrandisment and self-adulation. This in itself could mask a basic dissatisfaction with the way that things are turning out, for the Lion that takes this route is certainly unhappy in some way. Where the Leo truly understands human nature, inside as well as without, there is a balance that encourages the nature to shine out like the Sun. Knowing 'self', and changing those aspects that don't suit, is probably the greatest lesson that Leos have to learn on their path through life.

YOUR VIRTUES

Leos need to be special, in fact it is what makes them unique as individuals, a requirement that is shot through them as surely as the word Blackpool travels all the way through a stick of rock. However, working at their best, this individuality is sought outside in the real world and there Leos opt for glamour, opulent surroundings and any situation that is regal, magnificent and larger than life. The Lion's world must have drama and more than a splash of colour. This is a vast playground full of wonderful experiments and it is an environment that the Leo is more than happy to share with the people who come along for the ride.

With eloquent gestures and an aura of nobility, the Lion seeks to make the world a better place for everyone, for there is no inherent selfishness here and the Leo expounds a belief in democracy, as long as he or she can set the constitution. One of the more appealing qualities to be noticed about Leo is their boldness and courage when faced with obstacles that would deter or at the least intimidate a weaker sort of person. Part of this is down to the fact that Leo is a Fixed sign and as such stubbornly refuses to give in. The same fixity leads to a rather traditional streak, emphasising also the more showy qualities in terms of pageant or display.

In love, Leo is loyal and usually unswerving in terms of both loyalty and affection. The average Lion would move mountains for their chosen and cherished partner. Leos have no problem about being depended on, and in fact will encourage the tendency where a lover or family members are concerned; not really surprising because this child of the Sun loves to manage the show. The only time that they are happier still is when they occupy centre-stage, even if it is only for a short while, for Leo needs to let that little light shine more than any other sign of the zodiac. Between humility that doesn't suit them in any way, shape or form and rank self-worship, this is the place for Leos to be.

YOUR VICES

One of the more unattractive facets of Leo lies in their refusal to acknowledge the achievements of others, which can be infuriating, since it gives the impression that these people believe they have the monopoly on talent. It is in the nature of at least unawakened Leos to disregard potential competition in this way, since it irks them to think that any other person could do anything better than they can. It might be said in fact that at least a part of the apparently happy-go-lucky smile of the Leo is covering a basic lack of self-confidence, no matter what the manner seems to say to the contrary. Leo needs constant approbation to be even remotely secure and can turn sour if it isn't forthcoming.

Other vices stem from Leos exaggerated sense of self-importance. Here we find the labels 'pompous', 'snobbish', and 'condescending'. At its worst the Lion can be very patronising, treating the rest of humanity as little more than children, so apparently confident is the sign of its own superior powers. Hidden below this of course is the child within the Leo, crying out for the attention that it so badly needs. In some ways the Lion needs to grow upwards and outwards, seeing the world as a school-room and not as its own play-thing.

There are also Leos who cannot learn to forgive and forget, since the Leonine fixity can force them to carry a grudge around for half a lifetime. Yet the powerful feline energy here should not be inverted, lest the Leo fall victim to his own swollen pride. When not dealt with properly this can turn into ego-inflation of the worst possible sort. But who is there around powerful enough to convince the Leo that he or she is ultimately the same as other human beings? True enough, Leo is an individual, but then who isn't; and even monarchs have to serve the needs of their subjects at some time.

LIVING A HAPPY LIFE

In many respects you have it all. There are some signs of the zodiac that would give their right hands to have your confidence, courage and popularity. But it really is a matter of how you feel about your own life; after all, nobody lives inside your world except for you, and only you know the furniture of your own mental and spiritual dining room. Your constitution is generally strong, though in late middle age especially it is worth remembering that Leo rules the heart, so excessive drinking, smoking or eating really won't be much of a help in your search for longevity. Personally, you need the sort of partner that needs you, a simple formula that invariably works, for what is the Leo who has nobody to rely on them? .

You are an individual, and it isn't too far away from the truth to say that they threw the mould away when your sign was cast in the celestial foundry. Keep an eye on expenditure because your own natural generosity could leave you a little short from time to time. Despite this you have the ability to be successful and to earn what you need to be comfortable. Yours is a naturally happy life as long as you are fulfilled.

WHAT'S RISING

YOUR RISING SIGN AND PERSONALITY

Perhaps you have come across this term 'Rising Sign' when looking at other books on astrology and may have been somewhat puzzled as to what it actually means. To those not accustomed to astrological jargon it could sound somewhat technical and mysterious, though in fact, in terms of your own personal birth chart, it couldn't be simpler. The Rising Sign is simply that part of the zodiac occupying the eastern horizon at the time of your birth. Because it is a little more difficult to discover than your sun-sign, many writers of popular astrology have tended to ignore it, which is a great shame, because, together with the Sun, your Rising Sign is the single most important factor in terms of setting your personality. So much so, that no appraisal of your astrological nature could be complete without it.

Your Rising Sign, also known as your 'Ascendant' or 'Ascending Sign' plays a great part in your looks - yes, astrology can even predict what you are going to be like physically. In fact, this is a very interesting point, because there appears to be a tie-in between astrology and genetics. Professional Astrologers for centuries have noted the close relationship that often exists between the astrological birth chart of parents and those of their offspring, so that, if you look like your Mother or Father, chances are that there is a close astrological tie-up. Rising signs especially appear to be handed down through families.

The first impression that you get, in an astrological sense, upon meeting a stranger, is not related to their sun-sign but to the zodiac sign that was rising at the moment they came into the world. The Rising Sign is particularly important because it modifies the way that you display your Sun-sign to the world at large. A good example of this might be that of Britain's best-known ex- Prime minister, Margaret Thatcher. This dynamic and powerful lady is a Libran by Sun-sign placing, indicating a light-hearted nature, pleasure loving and very flexible. However, Mrs Thatcher has Scorpio as her Rising Sign, bringing a steely determination and a tremendous capacity for work. It also bestows an iron will and the power to thrive under pressure.

Here lies the true importance of the Rising Sign, for Mr Thatcher almost certainly knows a woman who most other people do not. The Rising Sign is a protective shell, and not until we know someone quite well do we start to discover the Sun-sign nature that hides within this often tough outer coat of astrological making. Your Rising Sign also represents your basic self-image, the social mask that is often so useful; and even if you don't think that you conform to the interpretation of your Ascendant, chances are that other people will think that you do.

The way that an individual looks, walks, sits and generally presents themselves to the world is all down to the Rising Sign. For example, a person possessed of Gemini Rising is apt to be very quick, energetic in all movements, deliberate in mannerisms and with a cheerful disposition. A bearer of a Taurean Ascendant on the other hand would probably not be so tall, more solid generally, quieter in aspect and calmer in movement. Once you come to understand the basics of astrology it is really very easy to pick out the Rising Signs of people that you come across, even though the Sun-sign is often more difficult to pin down. Keep an eye open for the dynamic and positive Aries Rising individual, or the retiring, shy but absolutely magnetic quality of of the Piscean Ascendant. Of course, in astrology, nothing is quite that simple. The position of a vast array of heavenly bodies at the time of birth also has to be taken into account, particularly that of the Moon and the inner planets Mercury and Venus. Nevertheless a knowledge of your Rising sign can be an invaluable aid in getting to know what really makes you tick as an individual.

To ascertain the exact degree of your Rising sign takes a little experience and recourse to some special material. However, I have evolved a series of tables that will enable you to discover at a glance what your Rising Sign is likely to be. All you need to know is the approximate time of your birth. At the back of the book you will find the necessary table related to your Sun-sign. Simply look down the left-hand column until you find your approximate time of birth, am or pm. Now scan across the top of the table to the place where your date of birth is shown. Look for the square where the two pieces of information connect and there is your Rising Sign. Now that you know what your Rising Sign is, read on, and learn even more about the fascinating interplay of astrological relationship.

LEO WITH LEO RISING

Having Leo as your Rising sign and your Sun-sign means that you were born around dawn, and is especially important in your case since your ruling planet in an astrological sense is the Sun anyway. There is no doubting your Leo pedigree, or that you are in almost every respect typical of your sign. This means that you are a good natured, philosophical sort of a person, generous by nature and kind-hearted in your associations with other people. When your interests and sympathy are aroused there is virtually no length that you would avoid in order to be of assistance to another individual.

On the reverse side of the coin, because you are a Fire sign, there are occasions when your temper could get the better of you and some care is necessary over impetuosity and the'highly strung' quality of your personality. However, even on those occasions when you might go over the top in your reactions. you do not bear a grudge for long and can be guaranteed to be smiling quite quickly. Friends are not difficult for you to find because you have a natural warmth that allows you to attract others to you, and once you make a friend, they are likely to stick around for a long time.

LEO WITH VIRGO RISING

There is a tremendous contrast between the two adjacent signs of Leo and Virgo, which is why you might have noticed that in many respects you are not like a Leo subject at all. Leo is outstanding and dynamic, whereas Virgo is quiet and sometimes even retiring. The light of the Sun, so obvious in the typical Leo subject, in your case is somewhat hidden under the bushel of responsibility and duty that Virgo places over it. On occasions it will show, probably in those social encounters when you feel at ease with yourself and your surroundings, though there is little doubt that under most circumstances, it is the quieter, more composed Virgo exterior that is on display.

You will always need to be busy doing something, and at first this looks like the Lion at work. However, yours is a measured response, more methodical and possibly a little too 'fussy' for your own good on occasions. It is very important that you don't allow yourself to get into a rut because if you do, the real you is bound to become very frustrated.

LEO WITH LIBRA RISING

The combination of Fire and Air evident in this matching of Sun and Rising sign can make for a very comfortable and rewarding combination. It is true that some people may find you to be just a touch fickle and this might make them somewhat reticent to be totally honest with you. You may also find it less than easy to take other people's feelings seriously, though in the main you focus on the lighter side of life, being refreshing to know and happy to be the sort of person that the zodiac has made you. Originality is the key as far as your nature is concerned and you take delight in anything that is out of the ordinary.

One of your most noticeable traits is the need you have of other people. Both Leo and Libra are very sociable signs and love the interplay that comes from groups or associations. You need colour, verve and excitement in your life in order to stay happy, though because Libra is ruled by Venus, you also require a certain degree of harmony and the beauty that you can bring to your surroundings. In company you are polite and courteous, you win arguments with a mixture of determination and diplomacy and probably have a hate of creating embarrassment for anyone.

LEO WITH SCORPIO RISING

Nobody would ever accuse you of being a shrinking violet. It is your subconscious consideration that you were put upon this earth to make the biggest impression possible and that is precisely what you set out to do. Everything that you undertake is directly stamped with your own indelible mark, you are powerful and intense, and it would take a brave person to tell you what you ought to do. This combination of Leo and Scorpio strengthens the ego no end. Fortunately the Leo component makes you interesting to listen to, which is just as well because you certainly are not shy when it comes to making your feelings known.

The combination of Fire and Water makes it difficult for you to distance yourself from any situation that is of personal importance. This means that for much of the time you are living life to the full and can put certain strains upon yourself as a result.

13

LEO WITH SAGITTARIUS RISING

The most obvious characteristics of this pairing of signs are restlessness, exuberance, chattiness, optimism and humour. Most people like what they see in you; let's face it, you are very easy to get on with, in a superficial sense at least. You are a double Fire sign, good for getting what you want out of life, provided that you don't take it too seriously, which for most of the time you do not. You could display some dislike of specifics, preferring in the main to take a bird's-eye view of life, an over-all scan that allows you an instinctive view of all situations. Life is a game to be played as far as you are concerned and you make up the rules as you go along.

Because Sagittarius is also a Fire sign, those who know about astrology would have you marked down as being a Leo almost from first impressions. As with Leo alone, you are cheerful, excitable and enthusiastic for new projects and anything that stimulates your intellect. The sign of the Archer could make you a little too outspoken for your own good on occasions, a fact that could get you into hot water from time to time. Subtle you are not, though your honesty itself can be refreshing to most types. The problem is that you express an opinion - and that can bring opposition as well as enthusiasm from others.

LEO WITH CAPRICORN RISING

Superior may be the best description of you, because your occasionally stubborn, egocentric personality can put other people's noses out of joint. Both the signs involved are self conscious and eager to find power in their own respective ways. This desire for power really means personal inner strength, though all too often can seem like awkwardness when viewed through the eyes of others. But it also brings the most complete form of determination, and perhaps success. You will work long and hard to see things work out the way that you want them to and only come out of difficult situations stronger, even more determined to find your own version of fulfilment.

Not that you are the type of person who manages to go through life without any form of self-doubt; you might be more content with yourself and the world at large if you could. All in all you are a fairly complex character and not at all easy for the average person to understand.

LEO WITH AQUARIUS RISING

These are two really odd bedfellows, though despite the fact you have much going for you. For a start the whole world is your friend, even those people that the rest of humanity finds difficult to take. In a general sense this makes for good social contacts and some success. Unfortunately, personal relationships could be a different matter. Aquarius Rising means that you feel yourself to be rather different from the norm, as if you are in the world but not of it. This is not so surprising when it is realised that Aquarians generally are in tune with humanity as a whole but less comfortable at an individual level.

Despite the restrictions that can occur personally, you have a keen sense of fair play and are very philanthropic in your attitude to life. In order to tip the balance back in your favour from a one-to-one point of view, it is important for you to look for an opposite number who represents normality, rather than the rather extraordinary type of person who may instinctively appear to be so attractive.

LEO WITH PISCES RISING

With any Fire-Water combination there are various things to bear in mind when approaching the world. For example it is easy to fall into the trap of believing that everyone else thinks the same way that you do. If you continue indefinitely with this philosophy it is only a matter of time before you are going to have your eyes opened by circumstances, which can be a very hurtful experience. A certain characteristic of yours is your ability to be led astray by the excitement and glamour of the moment, only to have to wake up to the hard facts of life later on. You have a slightly over-idealistic view of the world and need to ensure that you keep in touch with reality in all your dealings with the big, bad world outside your own door. Your vivid imagination needs to be given the proper channels to make the most of this quality, while your Leo side achieves practical results and should ensure success in business. Relationships can be something of a problem, simply because of your rather unique view of reality. You need a practical partner, though you also revel in romance and respond well to compliments and the sort of constancy that, in your worst moments, you can lack yourself.

LEO WITH ARIES RISING

The small 'i', that psychologists refer to as the ego, does not exist in your approach to life, for if ever a combination of Rising and Sun signs created a capital 'I' personality, it has done so in your case. You really do find it difficult to believe that others can think differently, and almost impossible to accept that your way of doing things may not be theirs. This is a meeting of two very powerful Fire signs, and as such, the softly-softly touch is very important on your part to make certain that you do not tread on too many toes. In many respects you are a medieval monarch or an Egyptian Pharaoh, born out of your time and place, though in fairness you personify this type of person in positive as well as negative ways.

It is true that you relish the attention that your regal bearing demands but you also take on board a responsibility for the people in your vicinity and will fight extremely hard for any cause that you believe in. You don't care for interference to your plans and ambitions and can get through the kind of obstacles that might stop a tank in its tracks.

LEO WITH TAURUS RISING

In many ways you are quite untypical of your Sun sign of Leo because the more methodical and careful tendencies of Taurus run contrary to the dynamism and drive of Leo. This means that there is a pronounced conflict of interests between the two aspects of your nature, which need by no means be a problem, if it is utilised correctly, and can lead to much material success, something that is very important to you. In most projects you move forward like a steam-roller, slow to get moving but impossible to stop once it does. Of course, you don't care very much for the unexpected when it occurs and so are better following lines that involve little in the way of chance and owe much to the hard worker that you are.

Because you are so affectionate by nature, it would be difficult for anyone to dislike you. In fact your popularity is a very important factor, since it is grist to the mill of personal success, as well as a means of finding ways to help others, which you are also quite willing to do. A real danger with your nature is that you may become so fixed in your routines that you can even make your own life boring.

LEO WITH GEMINI RISING

This combination of Air and Fire offers you a number of advantages over others, since you possess qualities which are much esteemed in modern society. Firstly, you have the power to communicate successfully, courtesy of your quick brain. In addition, you have a good sense of humour, a facet that means you are rarely short of company. Certainly you are a social animal, and yet people often find it difficult to know where they stand with you, simply because you are so changeable. The trouble is that the whole of life is of interest to you and why should you limit yourself to only one person when the world offers so much?

Important matters can be totally disregarded on occasions, a tendency that you should try to counter with a little more conditioned persistence. It isn't that you find it impossible to see things through to the end, merely that you cannot be bothered to do so. Being tied down may not be your style, though as long as you manage to have variety in your life you can stick to a degree of convention as well as anyone else. Commanding attention is easy for you.

LEO WITH CANCER RISING

Classical astrology considered the combination of Fire and Water that is brought together here would make for a temperamental nature, and though this is true to a certain extent, you have much going for you and can turn the various facets of your nature to your advantage. There is no doubt that you have your heart in the right place, all Cancerian Rising signs do, Add to this the warmth of Leo and we find an aversion to coldness in others that may rank as your highest quality. You do need someone or something to look after and are quite able to watch out for other's personal needs. The only thing that you ask in return is a little gratitude but woe betide the object of your attention if you don't get it!

Look out for wild impulses, doing your best to squash the natural tendency to jump in at the deep end, only to discover that you can't swim as well as you thought. What you really have to learn is to stand back and take a dispassionate view of the world, sometimes stifling your 'feelings' in an attempt to see things rationally. Like all Leos, you seek to impress.

LEO
IN LOVE AND FRIENDSHIP

WANT TO KNOW HOW WELL YOU GET ON WITH OTHER ZODIAC SIGNS?

THE TABLES BELOW DEAL WITH LOVE AND FRIENDSHIP

THE MORE HEARTS THERE ARE AGAINST ANY SIGN OF THE ZODIAC, THE BETTER THE CHANCE OF CUPID'S DART SCORING A DIRECT HIT.

THE SMILES OF FRIENDSHIP DISPLAY HOW WELL YOU WORK OR ASSOCIATE WITH ALL THE OTHER SIGNS OF THE ZODIAC.

Love					Sign	Friendship				
♥	♥	♥	♥	♥	ARIES	☺	☺	☺	☺	☺
		♥	♥	♥	TAURUS	☺	☺			
			♥	♥	GEMINI	☺	☺	☺		
			♥	♥	CANCER	☺	☺	☺		
♥	♥	♥	♥	♥	LEO	☺	☺	☺	☺	☺
			♥	♥	VIRGO	☺	☺	☺		
		♥	♥	♥	LIBRA	☺	☺	☺		
		♥	♥	♥	SCORPIO	☺	☺			
♥	♥	♥	♥	♥	SAGITTARIUS	☺	☺	☺	☺	☺
			♥	♥	CAPRICORN	☺	☺			
				♥	AQUARIUS	☺	☺			
	♥	♥	♥	♥	PISCES	☺	☺	☺	☺	

THE MOON AND YOUR DAY-TO-DAY LIFE

Look up at the sky on cloudless nights and you are almost certain to see the Earth's closest neighbour in space, engaged in her intricate and complicated relationship with the planet upon which we live. The Moon isn't very large, in fact only a small fraction of the size of the Earth, but it is very close to us in spatial terms, and here lies the reason why the Moon probably has more of a part to play in your day-to-day life than any other body in space.

It is fair to say in astrological terms that if the Sun and Planets represent the hour and minute hands regulating your character swings and mood changes, the Moon is a rapidly sweeping second hand, governing emotions especially, but touching practically every aspect of your life.

Although the Moon moves so quickly, and maintains a staggeringly complex orbital relationship with the Earth, no book charting the possible ups and downs of your daily life could be complete without some reference to lunar action. For this reason I have included a number of the more important lunar cycles that you can observe within your own life, and also give you the opportunity to discover which zodiac sign the Moon occupied when you were born. Follow the instructions below and you will soon have a far better idea of where astrological cycles come from, and the part they play in your life.

SUN MOON CYCLES

The first lunar cycle deals with the relationship that the Moon keeps with your Sun sign. I have made the fluctuations of this pattern easy for you to understand by means of a simple cyclic graph. It appears on the first page of each 'Your Month At A Glance', under the title 'Highs and Lows'. The graph displays the lunar cycle and you will soon learn to understand how its movements have a bearing on your level of energy and your abilities. Once you recognise the patterns, you can work within them, making certain that your maximum efforts are expounded at the most opportune time.

MOON AGE CYCLES

Looking at the second lunar pattern that helps to make you feel the way you do, day-to-day, involves a small amount of work on your part to establish how you slot into the rhythm. However, since Moon Age cycles are one of the most potent astrological forces at work in your life, the effort is more than worthwhile.

This cycle refers to the way that the date of your birth fits into the Moon Phase pattern. Because of the complex relationship of the Earth and the Moon, we see the face of the lunar disc change throughout a period of roughly one month. The time between one New Moon (this is when there is no Moon to be seen) to the next New Moon, is about 29 days. Between the two the Moon would have seemed larger each night until the lunar disc was Full; it would then start to recede back towards New again. We call this cycle the Moon Age Cycle and classify the day of the New Moon as day 0. Full Moon occurs on day 15 with the last day of the cycle being either day 28 or day 29, dependent on the complicated motions of the combined Earth and Moon.

If you know on what Moon Age Day you were born, then you also know how you fit into the cycle. You would monitor the changes of the cycle as more or less tension in your body, an easy or a strained disposition, good or bad temper and so forth. In order to work out your Moon Age Day follow the steps below:

STEP 1: Look at the two New Moon Tables on pages 23 and 24. Down the left hand column you will see every year from 1902 to 1994 listed, and the months of the year appear across the top. Where the year of your birth and the month that you were born coincide, the figure shown indicates the date of the month on which New Moon occurred.

STEP 2: You need to pick the New Moon that occurred prior to your day of birth, so if your birthday falls at the beginning of the month, you may have to refer to the New Moon from the previous month. Once you have established the nearest New Moon prior to your birthday, (and of course in the correct year), all you have to do is count forward to your birthday. (Don't forget that the day of the New Moon is classed as 0.) As an example, if your were born on March 22nd 1962, the last New Moon before your birthday would have occurred on 6th March 1962. Counting forward from 6 to 22 would mean that you were born on Moon Age

Day 16. If your Moon Phase Cycle crosses the end of February, don't forget to check whether or not you were born in a Leap Year. If so you will have to compensate for that fact.

HOW TO USE MOON AGE DAYS

Once you know your Moon Age Day, you can refer to the Diary section of the book, because there, on each day of the year, you will see that the Moon Age Day is listed. The day in each cycle that conforms to your own Moon Age monthly birthday should find you in a positive and optimistic frame of mind Your emotions are likely to be settled and your thinking processes clear and concise. There are other important days that you will want to know about on this cycle, and to make matters simpler I have compiled an easy to follow table on pages 25 and 26. Quite soon you will get to know which Moon Age Days influence you, and how.

Of course Moon Age Cycles, although specific to your own date of birth, also run within the other astrological patterns that you will find described in this book. So, for example, if your Moon Age Day coincided with a particular day of the month, but everything else was working to the contrary, you might be wise to delay any particularly monumental effort until another, more generally favourable, day. Sometimes cycles run together and occasionally they do not; this is the essence of astrological prediction.

YOUR MOON SIGN

Once you have established on what Moon Age Day you were born, it isn't too difficult to also discover what zodiac sign the Moon occupied on the day of your birth. Although the Moon is very small in size compared to some of the solar system's larger bodies, it is very close indeed to the Earth and this seems to give it a special astrological significance. This is why there are many cycles and patterns associated with the Moon that have an important part to play in the lives of every living creature on the face of our planet, Of all the astrological patterns associated with the Moon that have a part to play in your life, none is more potent than those related to the zodiac position of the Moon at birth. Many of the most intimate details of your personal make-up are related to your Moon Sign, and we will look at these now.

HOW TO DISCOVER YOUR MOON SIGN

The Moon moves through each sign of the zodiac in only two to three days. It also has a rather complicated orbital relationship with the Earth; for these reasons it can be difficult to work out what your Zodiac Moon Sign is. However, having discovered your Moon Age Day you are half way towards finding your Moon Sign, and in order to do so, simply follow the steps below:

STEP 1: Make sure that you have a note of your date of birth and also your Moon Age Day.

STEP 2: Look at Zodiac Moon Sign Table 1 on page 27. Find the month of your birth across the top of the table, and your date of birth down the left. Where the two converge you will see a letter. Make a note of the letter that relates to you.

STEP 3: Now turn to Zodiac Moon Sign Table 2 on pages 28 and 30. Look for your Moon Age Day across the top of the tables and the letter that you have just discoverd down the left side. Where the two converge you will see a zodiac sign. The Moon occupied this zodiac sign on the day of your birth.

PLEASE NOTE: The Moon can change signs at any time of the day or night, and the signs listed in this book are generally applicable for 12 noon on each day. If you were born near the start or the end of a particular Zodiac Moon Sign, it is worth reading the character descriptions of adjacent signs. These are listed pages 30to 35. So much of your nature is governed by the Moon at the time of your birth that it should be fairly obvious wich one of the profiles relates to you.

YOUR ZODIAC MOON SIGN EXPLAINED

You will find a profile of all Zodiac Moon Signs on pages 30 to 35, showing in yet another way astrology helps to make you into the individual that you are. In each month in the Astral Diary, in addition to your Moon Age Day, you can also discover your Zodiac Moon Sign birthday (that day when the Moon occupies the same zodiac sign as it did when you were born). At these times you are in the best postion to be emotionally steady and to make the sort of decisions that have real, lasting value.

NEW MOON TABLE

YEAR	JAN	FEB	MAR	APR	MAY	JUN	JUL	AUG	SEP	OCT	NOV	DEC
1902	9	8	9	8	7	6	5	3	2	1/30	29	29
1903	27	26	28	27	26	25	24	22	21	20	19	18
1904	17	15	17	16	15	14	14	12	10	18	8	8
1905	6	5	5	4	3	2	2/31	30	28	28	26	26
1906	24	23	24	23	22	21	20	19	18	17	16	15
1907	14	12	14	12	11	10	9	8	7	6	5	5
1908	3	2	3	2	1/30	29	28	27	25	25	24	24
1909	22	20	21	20	19	17	17	15	14	14	13	12
1910	11	9	11	9	9	7	6	5	3	2	1	1/30
1911	29	28	30	28	28	26	25	24	22	21	20	20
1912	18	17	19	18	17	16	15	13	12	11	9	9
1913	7	6	7	6	5	4	3	2/31	30	29	28	27
1914	25	24	26	24	24	23	22	21	19	19	17	17
1915	15	14	15	13	13	12	11	10	9	8	7	6
1916	5	3	5	3	2	1/30	30	29	27	27	26	25
1917	24	22	23	22	20	19	18	17	15	15	14	13
1918	12	11	12	11	10	8	8	6	4	4	3	2
1919	1/31	-	2/31	30	29	27	27	25	23	23	22	21
1920	21	19	20	18	18	16	15	14	12	12	10	10
1921	9	8	9	8	7	6	5	3	2	1/30	29	29
1922	27	26	28	27	26	25	24	22	21	20	19	18
1923	17	15	17	16	15	14	14	12	10	10	8	8
1924	6	5	5	4	3	2	2/31	30	28	28	26	26
1925	24	23	24	23	22	21	20	19	18	17	16	15
1926	14	12	14	12	11	10	9	8	7	6	5	5
1927	3	2	3	2	1/30	29	28	27	25	25	24	24
1928	21	19	21	20	19	18	17	16	14	14	12	12
1929	11	9	11	9	9	7	6	5	3	2	1	1/30
1930	29	28	30	28	28	26	25	24	22	20	20	19
1931	18	17	19	18	17	16	15	13	12	11	9	9
1932	7	6	7	6	5	4	3	2/31	30	29	2	27
1933	25	24	26	24	24	23	22	21	19	19	17	17
1934	15	14	15	13	13	12	11	10	9	8	7	6
1935	5	3	5	3	2	1/30	30	29	27	27	26	25
1936	24	22	23	21	20	19	18	17	15	15	14	13
1937	12	11	12	12	10	8	8	6	4	4	3	2
1938	1/31	-	2/31	30	29	27	27	25	23	23	22	21
1939	20	19	20	19	19	17	16	15	13	12	11	10
1940	9	8	9	7	7	6	5	4	2	1/30	29	28
1941	27	26	27	26	26	24	24	22	21	20	19	18
1942	16	15	16	15	15	13	13	12	10	10	8	8
1943	6	4	6	4	4	2	2	1/30	29	29	27	27
1944	25	24	24	22	22	20	20	18	17	17	15	15
1945	14	12	14	12	11	10	9	8	6	6	4	4
1946	3	2	3	2	1/30	29	28	26	25	24	23	23
1947	21	19	21	20	19	18	17	16	14	14	12	12

NEW MOON TABLE

YEAR	JAN	FEB	MAR	APR	MAY	JUN	JUL	AUG	SEP	OCT	NOV	DEC
1948	11	9	11	9	9	7	6	5	3	2	1	1/30
1949	29	27	29	28	27	26	25	24	23	21	20	19
1950	18	16	18	17	17	15	15	13	12	11	9	9
1951	7	6	7	6	6	4	4	2	1	1/30	29	28
1952	26	25	25	24	23	22	23	20	29	28	27	27
1953	15	14	15	13	13	11	11	9	8	8	6	6
1954	5	3	5	3	2	1/30	29	28	27	26	25	25
1955	24	22	24	22	21	20	19	17	16	15	14	14
1956	13	11	12	11	10	8	8	6	4	4	2	2
1957	1/30	-	1/31	29	29	27	27	25	23	23	21	21
1958	19	18	20	19	18	17	16	15	13	12	11	10
1959	9	7	9	8	7	6	6	4	3	2/31	30	29
1960	27	26	27	26	26	24	24	22	21	20	19	18
1961	16	15	16	15	14	13	12	11	10	9	8	7
1962	6	5	6	5	4	2	1/31	30	28	28	27	26
1963	25	23	25	23	23	21	20	19	17	17	15	15
1964	14	13	14	12	11	10	9	7	6	5	4	4
1965	3	1	2	1	1/30	29	28	26	25	24	22	22
1966	21	19	21	20	19	18	17	16	14	14	12	12
1967	10	9	10	9	8	7	7	5	4	3	2	1/30
1968	29	28	29	28	27	26	25	24	23	22	21	20
1969	1 9	17	18	16	15	14	13	12	11	10	9	9
1970	7	6	7	6	6	4	4	2	1	1/30	29	28
1971	26	25	26	25	24	22	22	20	19	19	18	17
1972	15	14	15	13	13	11	11	9	8	8	6	6
1973	5	4	5	3	2	1/30	29	28	27	26	25	25
1974	24	22	24	22	21	20	19	17	16	15	14	14
1975	12	11	12	11	11	9	9	7	5	5	3	3
1976	1/31	29	30	29	29	27	27	25	23	23	21	21
1977	19	18	19	18	18	16	16	14	13	12	11	10
1978	9	7	9	7	7	5	5	4	2	2/31	30	29
1979	27	26	27	26	26	24	24	22	21	20	19	18
1980	16	15	16	15	14	13	12	11	10	9	8	7
1981	6	4	6	4	4	2	1/31	29	28	27	26	26
1982	25	23	24	23	21	21	20	19	17	17	15	15
1983	14	13	14	13	12	11	10	8	7	6	4	4
1984	3	1	2	1	1/30	29	28	26	25	24	22	22
1985	21	19	21	20	19	18	17	16	14	14	12	12
1986	10	9	10	9	8	7	7	5	4	3	2	1/30
1987	29	28	29	28	27	26	25	24	23	22	21	20
1988	19	17	18	16	15	14	13	12	11	10	9	9
1989	7	6	7	6	5	3	3	1/31	29	29	28	28
1990	26	25	26	25	24	22	22	20	19	18	17	17
1991	15	14	15	13	13	11	11	9	8	8	6	6
1992	4	3	4	3	2	1/30	29	28	26	25	24	24
1993	24	22	24	22	21	20	19	17	16	15	14	14
1994	11	10	12	11	10	9	8	7	5	5	3	2

MOON AGE QUICK REFERENCE TABLE

SIGNIFICANT MOON AGE DAYS

		+ Days	- Days	* Days
	0	4, 6, 12, 14, 19, 21, 25, 28	9, 16, 23	0
	1	5, 7, 13, 15, 20, 22, 26, 29	10, 17, 24	1
	2	0, 6, 8, 14, 16, 21, 23, 27	11, 18, 25	2
	3	1, 7, 9, 15, 17, 22, 24, 28	12, 19, 26	3
	4	2, 8, 10, 16, 18, 23, 25, 29	13, 20, 27	4
Y	5	0, 3, 4, 9, 11, 17, 19, 24, 26	14, 21, 28	5
O	6	1, 4, 5, 10, 12, 18, 20, 25, 27	15, 22, 29	6
U R	7	2, 5, 11, 13, 19, 21, 26, 28	0, 16, 23	7
	8	3, 6, 12, 14, 20, 22, 27, 29	1, 17, 24	8
O	9	0, 4, 7, 13, 15, 21, 23, 28	2, 18, 25	9
W N	10	1, 5, 8, 14, 16, 22, 24, 29	3, 19, 26	10
	11	0, 2, 6, 9, 15, 17, 23, 25	4, 20, 27	11
M	12	1, 3, 7, 10, 16, 18, 24, 26	5, 21, 28	12
O O	13	2, 4, 8, 11, 17, 19, 25, 27	6, 22, 29	13
N	14	3, 5, 9, 12, 18, 20, 26, 28	0, 7, 23	14
	15	4, 6, 10, 13, 19, 21, 27, 29	1, 8, 24	15
A	16	0, 5, 7, 11, 14, 20, 22, 28	2, 9, 25	16
G E	17	1, 6, 8, 12, 15, 21, 23, 29	3, 10, 26	17
	18	0, 2, 7, 9, 13, 16, 22, 24	4, 11, 27	18
D	19	1, 3, 8, 10, 14, 17, 23, 25	5, 12, 28	19
A Y	20	2, 4, 9, 11, 15, 18, 24, 26	6, 13, 29	20
	21	3, 5, 10, 12, 16, 19, 25, 27	0, 7, 14	21
	22	4, 6, 11, 13, 17, 20, 26, 28	1, 8, 15	22
	23	5, 7, 12, 14, 18, 21, 27, 29	2, 9, 16	23
	24	0, 6, 8, 13, 15, 19, 22, 28	3, 10, 17	24
	25	1, 7, 9, 14, 16, 20, 23, 29	4, 11, 18	25
	26	0, 2, 8, 10, 15, 17, 21, 24,	5, 12, 19	26
	27	1, 3, 9, 11, 16, 18, 22, 25	6, 13, 20	27
	28	2, 4, 10, 12, 17, 19, 23, 26	7, 14, 21	28
	29	3, 5, 11, 13, 18, 20, 24, 27	8, 15, 22	29

MOON AGE QUICK REFERENCE TABLE

The table opposite will allow you to plot the significant days on the Moon Age Day Cycle and to monitor the way they have a bearing on your own life. You will find an explanation of the Moon Age Cycles on pages 20 - 22. Once you know your own Moon Age Day, you can find it in the left-hand column of the table opposite, To the right of your Moon Age Day you will observe a series of numbers; these appear under three headings. + Days, - Days and * Days.

If you look at the Diary section of the book, immediately to the right of each day and date, the Moon Age Day number is listed. The Quick Reference Table allows you to register which Moon Age Days are significant to you. For example: if your own Moon Age Day is 5, each month you should put a + in the Diary section against Moon Age Days 0, 3, 4, 9, 11, 17, 19, 24, and 26. Jot down a - against Moon Age Days 14, 21 and 28, and a * against Moon Age Day 5. You can now follow your own personal Moon Age Cycle every day of the year.

+ Days are periods when the Moon Age Cycle is in tune with your own Moon Age Day. At this time life should be more harmonious and your emotions are likely to be running smoothly. These are good days for making decisions.

- Days find the Moon Age Cycle out of harmony with your own Moon Age Day. Avoid taking chances at these times and take life reasonably steady. Confrontation would not make sense.

* Days occur only once each Moon Age Cycle, and represent your own Moon Age Day. Such times should be excellent for taking the odd chance and for moving positively towards your objectives in life. On those rare occasions where a * day coincides with your lunar high, you would really be looking at an exceptional period and could afford to be quite bold and adventurous in your approach to life.

MOON ZODIAC SIGN TABLE 1

	Month	Jan	Feb	Mar	Apr	May	Jun	Jul	Aug	Sep	Oct	Nov	Dec
	1	A	D	F	J	M	O	R	U	X	a	e	i
	2	A	D	G	J	M	P	R	U	X	a	e	i
	3	A	D	G	J	M	P	S	V	X	a	e	m
	4	A	D	G	J	M	P	S	V	Y	b	f	m
	5	A	D	G	J	M	P	S	V	Y	b	f	n
	6	A	D	G	J	M	P	S	V	Y	b	f	n
	7	A	D	G	J	M	P	S	V	Y	b	f	n
	8	A	D	G	J	M	P	S	V	Y	b	f	n
D	9	A	D	G	J	M	P	S	V	Y	b	f	n
A	10	A	E	G	J	M	P	S	V	Y	b	f	n
Y	11	B	E	G	K	M	P	S	V	Y	b	f	n
	12	B	E	H	K	N	Q	S	V	Y	b	f	n
O	13	B	E	H	K	N	Q	T	V	Y	b	g	n
F	14	B	E	H	K	N	Q	T	W	Z	d	g	n
	15	B	E	H	K	N	Q	T	W	Z	d	g	n
M	16	B	E	H	K	N	Q	T	W	Z	d	g	n
O	17	B	E	H	K	N	Q	T	W	Z	d	g	n
N	18	B	E	H	K	N	Q	T	W	Z	d	g	n
T	19	B	E	H	K	N	Q	T	W	Z	d	g	n
H	20	B	F	H	K	N	Q	T	W	Z	d	g	n
	21	C	F	H	L	N	Q	T	W	Z	d	g	n
	22	C	F	I	L	O	R	T	W	Z	d	g	n
	23	C	F	I	L	O	R	T	W	Z	d	i	q
	24	C	F	I	L	O	R	U	X	a	e	i	q
	25	C	F	I	L	O	R	U	X	a	e	i	q
	26	C	F	I	L	O	R	U	X	a	e	i	q
	27	C	F	I	L	O	R	U	X	a	e	i	q
	28	C	F	I	L	O	R	U	X	a	e	i	q
	29	C	-	I	L	O	R	U	X	a	e	i	q
	30	C	-	I	L	O	R	U	X	a	e	i	q
	31	D	–	I	-	O	-	U	X	-	e	-	q

27

Moon Age Day	0	1	2	3	4	5	6	7	8	9	10	11	12	13
A	Ca	Aq	Aq	Aq	Pi	Pi	Ar	Ar	Ar	Ta	Ta	Ge	Ge	Ge
B	Aq	Aq	Aq	Pi	Pi	Ar	Ar	Ar	Ta	Ta	Ge	Ge	Ge	Cn
C	Aq	Aq	Pi	Pi	Ar	Ar	Ar	Ta	Ta	Ge	Ge	Ge	Cn	Cn
D	Aq	Pi	Pi	Pi	Ar	Ar	Ta	Ta	Ta	Ge	Ge	Cn	Cn	Le
E	Pi	Pi	Pi	Ar	Ar	Ta	Ta	Ta	Ge	Ge	Cn	Cn	Cn	Le
F	Pi	Pi	Ar	Ar	Ar	Ta	Ta	Ge	Ge	Cn	Cn	Cn	Le	Le
G	Pi	Ar	Ar	Ar	Ta	Ta	Ge	Ge	Ge	Cn	Cn	Le	Le	Le
H	Ar	Ar	Ar	Ta	Ta	Ge	Ge	Ge	Cn	Cn	Le	Le	Le	Vi
I	Ar	Ar	Ta	Ta	Ge	Ge	Ge	Cn	Cn	Cn	Le	Le	Vi	Vi
J	Ar	Ta	Ta	Ta	Ge	Ge	Cn	Cn	Cn	Le	Le	Vi	Vi	Vi
K	Ta	Ta	Ta	Ge	Ge	Cn	Cn	Cn	Le	Le	Vi	Vi	Vi	Li
L	Ta	Ta	Ge	Ge	Ge	Cn	Cn	Le	Le	Vi	Vi	Vi	Li	Li
M	Ta	Ge	Ge	Ge	Cn	Cn	Le	Le	Le	Vi	Vi	Li	Li	Li
N	Ge	Ge	Ge	Cn	Cn	Le	Le	Le	Vi	Vi	Li	Li	Li	Sc
O	Ge	Ge	Cn	Cn	Cn	Le	Le	Vi	Vi	Li	Li	Sc	Sc	Sc
P	Ge	Cn	Cn	Cn	Le	Le	Vi	Vi	Vi	Li	Li	Sc	Sc	Sc
Q	Cn	Cn	Cn	Le	Le	Vi	Vi	Li	Li	Sc	Sc	Sc	Sa	Sa
R	Cn	Cn	Le	Le	Le	Vi	Vi	Li	Li	Li	Sc	Sc	Sa	Sa
S	Cn	Le	Le	Le	Vi	Vi	Li	Li	Li	Sc	Sc	Sa	Sa	Sa
T	Le	Le	Le	Vi	Vi	Li	Li	Li	Sc	Sc	Sa	Sa	Sa	Ca
U	Le	Le	Vi	Vi	Li	Li	Li	Sc	Sc	Sa	Sa	Ca	Ca	Ca
V	Le	Vi	Vi	Vi	Li	Li	Sc	Sc	Sc	Sa	Sa	Ca	Ca	Ca
W	Le	Vi	Vi	Li	Li	Sc	Sc	Sa	Sa	Sa	Ca	Ca	Aq	Aq
X	Vi	Vi	Li	Li	Li	Sc	Sc	Sa	Sa	Sa	Ca	Ca	Aq	Aq
Y	Vi	Li	Li	Li	Sc	Sc	Sa	Sa	Sa	Ca	Ca	Aq	Aq	Aq
Z	Li	Li	Li	Sc	Sc	Sc	Sa	Sa	Ca	Ca	Ca	Aq	Aq	Pi
a	Li	Li	Li	Sc	Sc	Sa	Sa	Sa	Ca	Ca	Aq	Aq	Pi	Pi
b	Li	Li	Sc	Sc	Sa	Sa	Ca	Ca	Ca	Aq	Aq	Pi	Pi	Ar
d	Li	Sc	Sc	Sc	Sa	Sa	Ca	Ca	Ca	Aq	Aq	Pi	Pi	Pi
e	Sc	Sc	Sc	Sa	Sa	Ca	Ca	Aq	Aq	Aq	Pi	Pi	Ar	Ar
f	Sc	Sc	Sa	Sa	Ca	Ca	Aq	Aq	Pi	Pi	Ar	Ar	Ta	Ta
g	Sc	Sa	Sa	Ca	Ca	Aq	Aq	Pi	Pi	Pi	Ar	Ar	Ta	Ta
i	Sa	Sa	Ca	Ca	Ca	Aq	Aq	Pi	Pi	Ar	Ar	Ta	Ta	Ge
m	Sa	Sa	Ca	Ca	Aq	Aq	Aq	Pi	Pi	Ar	Ar	Ta	Ta	Ge
n	Sa	Ca	Ca	Aq	Aq	Pi	Pi	Ar	Ar	Ta	Ta	Ta	Ge	Ge
q	Ca	Ca	Aq	Aq	Pi	Pi	Ar	Ar	Ar	Ta	Ta	Ge	Ge	Ge

(Left margin label: LETTER)

**Ar = Aries Ta = Taurus Ge = Gemini Cn = Cancer Le = Leo
Aq = Aquarius**

SIGN TABLE 2

14	15	16	17	18	19	20	21	22	23	24	25	26	27	28	29
Cn	Cn	Le	Le	Le	Vi	Vi	Li	Li	Li	Sc	Sc	Sa	Sa	Sa	Ca
Cn	Le	Le	Le	Vi	Vi	Li	Li	Li	Sc	Sc	Sa	Sa	Sa	Ca	Ca
Le	Le	Le	Vi	Vi	Vi	Li	Li	Sc	Sc	Sc	Sa	Sa	Ca	Ca	Ca
Le	Le	Vi	Vi	Vi	Li	Li	Sc	Sc	Sc	Sa	Sa	Ca	Ca	Aq	Aq
Le	Vi	Vi	Vi	Li	Li	Sc	Sc	Sc	Sa	Sa	Ca	Ca	Aq	Aq	Aq
Vi	Vi	Vi	Li	Li	Li	Sc	Sc	Sa	Sa	Sa	Ca	Ca	Aq	Aq	Aq
VI	Vi	Li	Li	Li	Sc	Sc	Sa	Sa	Sa	Ca	Ca	Aq	Aq	Aq	Pi
VI	Li	Li	Li	Sc	Sc	Sa	Sa	Sa	Ca	Ca	Aq	Aq	Aq	Pi	Pi
Li	Li	Li	Sc	Sc	Sc	Sa	Sa	Ca	Ca	Ca	Aq	Aq	Pi	Pi	Pi
Li	Li	Sc	Sc	Sc	Sa	Sa	Ca	Ca	Ca	Aq	Aq	Pi	Pi	Pi	Ar
Li	Sc	Sc	Sc	Sa	Sa	Ca	Ca	Ca	Aq	Aq	Pi	Pi	Pi	Ar	Ar
Li	Sc	Sc	Sa	Sa	Sa	Ca	Ca	Aq	Aq	Aq	Pi	Pi	Ar	Ar	Ar
Sc	Sc	Sa	Sa	Sa	Ca	Ca	Aq	Aq	Aq	Pi	Pi	Ar	Ar	Ar	Ta
Sc	Sa	Sa	Sa	Ca	Ca	Aq	Aq	Aq	Pi	Pi	Ar	Ar	Ar	Ta	Ta
Sa	Sa	Sa	Ca	Ca	Ca	Aq	Aq	Pi	Pi	Pi	Ar	Ar	Ta	Ta	Ta
Sa	Sa	Ca	Ca	Ca	Aq	Aq	Pi	Pi	Pi	Ar	Ar	Ta	Ta	Ta	Ge
Sa	Ca	Ca	Ca	Aq	Aq	Pi	Pi	Pi	Ar	Ar	Ta	Ta	Ta	Ge	Ge
Sa	Ca	Ca	Aq	Aq	Aq	Pi	Pi	Ar	Ar	Ar	Ta	Ta	Ge	Ge	Ge
Ca	Ca	Aq	Aq	Aq	Pi	Pi	Ar	Ar	Ar	Ta	Ta	Ge	Ge	Ge	Cn
Ca	Aq	Aq	Aq	Pi	Pi	Ar	Ar	Ar	Ta	Ta	Ge	Ge	Ge	Cn	Cn
Aq	Aq	Aq	Pi	Pi	Pi	Ar	Ar	Ta	Ta	Ta	Ge	Ge	Cn	Cn	Cn
Aq	Aq	Pi	Pi	Pi	Ar	Ar	Ta	Ta	Ta	Ge	Ge	Cn	Cn	Cn	Le
Pi	Pi	Pi	Pi	Ar	Ar	Ta	Ta	Ta	Ge	Ge	Cn	Cn	Cn	Le	Le
Pi	Pi	Pi	Ar	Ar	Ar	Ta	Ta	Ge	Ge	Ge	Cn	Cn	Le	Le	Le
Pi	Pi	Ar	Ar	Ar	Ta	Ta	Ge	Ge	Ge	Cn	Cn	Le	Le	Le	Vi
Pi	Pi	Ar	Ar	Ar	Ta	Ta	Ge	Ge	Ge	Cn	Cn	Le	Le	Le	Vi
Ar	Ar	Ar	Ar	Ta	Ta	Ge	Ge	Ge	Cn	Cn	Cn	Le	Le	Vi	Vi
Ar	Ar	Ar	Ta	Ta	Ta	Ge	Ge	Cn	Cn	Cn	Le	Le	Vi	Vi	Vi
Ar	Ar	Ta	Ta	Ge	Ge	Ge	Cn	Cn	Cn	Le	Le	Vi	Vi	Vi	Li
Ta	Ta	Ta	Ge	Ge	Ge	Cn	Cn	Cn	Le	Le	Le	Vi	Vi	Li	Li
Ge	Ta	Ge	Ge	Ge	Cn	Cn	Cn	Le	Le	Le	Vi	Vi	Li	Li	Li
Ge	Ta	Ge	Ge	Cn	Cn	Cn	Le	Le	Le	Vi	Vi	Li	Li	Li	Sc
Ge	Ge	Ge	Cn	Cn	Cn	Le	Le	Vi	Vi	Vi	Li	Li	Sc	Sc	Sc
Ge	Ge	Cn	Cn	Cn	Le	Le	Le	Vi	Vi	Vi	Li	Li	Sc	Sc	Sa
Cn	Ge	Cn	Cn	Le	Le	Le	Vi	Vi	Vi	Li	Li	Sc	Sc	Sc	Sa
Cn	Cn	Cn	Le	Le	Le	Vi	Vi	Li	Li	Li	Sc	Sc	Sa	Sa	Sa

**Vi = Virgo Li = Libra Sc = Scorpio Sa = Sagittarius Ca = Capricorn
Pi = Pisces**

MOON SIGNS

MOON IN ARIES

You have a strong imagination and a desire to do things in your own way. Showing no lack of courage you can forge your own path through life with great determination.

Originality is one of your most important attributes, you are seldom stuck for an idea though your mind is very changeable and more attention might be given over to one job at once. Few have the ability to order you around and you can be quite quick tempered. A calm and relaxed attitude is difficult for you to adopt but because you put tremendous pressure on your nervous system it is vitally important for you to forget about the cut and thrust of life from time to time. It would be fair to say that you rarely get the rest that you both need and deserve and becaue of this there is a chance that your health could break down from time to time.

Emotionally speaking you can be a bit of a mess if you don't talk to the folks that you are closest to and work out how you really feel about things. Once you discover that there are people willing to help you there is suddenly less necessity for trying to tackle everything yourself.

MOON IN TAURUS

The Moon in Taurus at the time you were born gives you a courteous and friendly manner that is likely to assure you of many friends.

The good things in life mean a great deal to you for Taurus is an Earth sign and delights in experiences that please the senses. This probably makes you a lover of good food and drink and might also mean that you have to spend time on the bathroom scales balancing the delight of a healthy appetite with that of looking good which is equally important to you.

Emotionally you are fairly stable and once you have opted for a set of standards you are inclined to stick to them because Taurus is a Fixed sign and doesn't respond particularly well to change. Intuition also plays an important part in your life.

MOON IN GEMINI

The Moon in the sign of Gemini gives a warm-hearted character, full of sympathy and usually ready to help those in difficulty. In some matters you are very reserved, whilst at other times you are articulate and chatty: this is part of the paradox of Gemini which always brings duplicity to the nature. The knowledge you possess of local and national affairs is very good, this strengthens and enlivens your intellect making you good company and endowing you with many friends. Most of the people with whom you mix have a high opinion of you and will stand ready to leap to your defence, not that this is generally necessary for although you are not martial by nature, you are more than capable of defending yourself verbally.

Travel plays an important part in your life and the naturally inquisitive quality of your mind allows you to benefit greatly from changes in scenery. The more you mix with people from different cultures and backgrounds the greater your interest in life becomes and intellectual stimulus is the meat and drink of the Gemini individual.

You can gain through reading and writing as well as the cultivation of artistic pursuits but you do need plenty of rest in order to avoid fatigue.

MOON IN CANCER

Moon in Cancer at the time of birth is a most fortunate position since the sign of Cancer is the Moon's natural home. This means that the qualities of compassion and understanding given by the Moon are especially enhanced in your nature and you cope quite well with emotional pressures that would bother others. You are friendly and sociably inclined. Domestic tasks don't really bother you and your greatest love is likely to be for home and family. Your surroundings are particularly important and you hate squalor and filth.

Your basic character, although at times changeable like the Moon itself, depends upon symmetry. Little wonder then that you are almost certain to have a love of music and poetry. Not surprising either that you do all within your power to make your surroundings comfortable and harmonious, not only for yourself, but on behalf of the folk who mean so much to you.

MOON IN LEO

You are especially ambitious and self-confident. The best qualities of both the Moon and the Sign of Leo come together here to ensure that you are warm-hearted and fair, characteristics that are almost certain to show through no matter what other planetary positions your chart contains.

You certainly don't lack the ability to organise, either yourself or those around you, and you invariably rise to a position of responsibility no matter what you decide to do with your life. Perhaps it is just as well because you don't enjoy being an'also ran' and would much rather be an important part of a small organisation than a menial in a larger one.

In love you are likely to be lucky and happy provided that youput in that extra bit of effort and you can be relied upon to build comfortable home surroundings for yourself and also those for whom you feel a particular responsibility. It is likely that you will have a love of pleasure and sport and perhaps a fondness for music and literature. Life brings you many rewards, though most of them are as a direct result of the effort that you are able to put in on your own behalf. All the same you are inclined to be more lucky than average and will usually make the best of any given circumstance.

MOON IN VIRGO

This position of the Moon endows you with good mental abilities and a keen receptive memory. By nature you are probably quite reserved, nevertheless you have many friends, especially of the opposite sex, and you gain a great deal as a result of these associations. Marital relationships need to be discussed carefully and kept as harmonious as possible because personal attachments can be something of a problem to you if sufficient attention is not given to the way you handle them.

You are not ostentatious or pretentious, two characteristics that are sure to improve your popularity. Talented and persevering you possess artistic qualities and are a good homemaker. Earning your honours through genuine merit you can work long and hard towards your objectives but probably show very little pride in your genuine achievements. Many short journeys will be undertaken in your life.

MOON IN LIBRA

With the Moon in Libra you have a popular nature and don't find it particularly difficult to make friends. Most folk like you, probably more than you think, and all get-together's would be more fun with you present. Libra, for all its good points, is not the most stable of astrological signs and as a result your emotions can prove to be a little unstable too. Although the Moon in Libra is generally said to be good for love and marriage, the position of the Sun, and also the Rising Sign, in your own birth chart will have a greater than usual bearing on your emotional and loving qualities.

You cannot live your life in isolation and must rely on other people, who are likely to play an important part in your decision making. Cooperation is crucial for you because Libra represents the 'balance' of life that can only be achieved through harmonious relationships. An offshoot of this fact is that you do not enjoy being disliked and, like all Librans are friendly to practically everybody.

Conformity is not always easy for you, because Libra is an Air sign and likes to go its own way.

MOON IN SCORPIO

Some people might call you a little pushy, in fact all you really want to do is live your life to the full, and to protect yourself and your family from the pressures of life that you recognise all too readily. You should avoid giving the impression of being sarcastic or too impulsive, at the same time using your energies wisely and in a constructive manner.

Nobody could doubt your courage which is great, and you invariably achieve what you set out to do, by force of personality as well as by the effort that you are able to put in. You are fond of mystery and are probably quite perceptive as to the outcome of situations and events.

Problems can arise in your relationships with members of the opposite sex, so before you commit yourself emotionally it is very important to examine your motives carefully and ensure that the little demon, jealousy, always a problem with Scorpio positions, does not cloud your judgement in love matches. You need to travel and can make gains as a result.

MOON IN SAGITTARIUS

The Moon is Sagittarius helps to make you a generous individual with humanitarian qualities and a kind heart. Restlessness may be an endemic part of your character for your mind is seldom still. Perhaps because of this you have an overwhelming need for change that could lead you to several major moves during your adult life. You are probably a reasonably sporting sort of person and not afraid to stand your ground on the occasions when you know that you are correct in your judgement. What you have to say goes right to the heart of the matter and your intuition is very good.

At work you are quick and efficient in whatever you choose to do, and because you are versatile you make an ideal employee. Ideally you need work that is intellectually demanding because you are no drudge and would not enjoy tedious routines. In relationships you anger quickly if faced with stupidity or deception, though you are just as quick to forgive and forget. Emotionally there are times when you allow your heart to rule your head.

MOON IN CAPRICORN

Born with the Moon in Capricorn, you are popular and may come into the public eye in one way or another. Your administrative ability is good and you are a capable worker. The watery Moon is not entirely at home in the Earth sign of Capricorn and as a result difficulties can be experienced, especially in the early years of life. Some initial lack of creative ability and indecision has to be overcome before the true qualities of patience and perseverance inherent in Capricorn can show through.

If caution is exercised in financial affairs you can accumulate wealth with the passing of time but you will always have to be careful about forming any partnerships because you are open to deception more than most. Under such circumstances you would be well-advised to gain professional advice before committing yourself. Many people with the Moon in Capricorn take a healthy interest in social or welfare work. The organisational skills that you have, together with a genuine sympathy for others, means that you are suited to this kind of career.

MOON IN AQUARIUS

With the Moon in Aquarius you are an active and agreeable person with a friendly easy going sort of nature. Being sympathetic to the needs of other people you flourish best in an easy going atmosphere. You are broad-minded, just, and open to suggestion, though as with all faces of Aquarius the Moon here brings an unconventional quality that not everyone would find easy to understand.

You have a liking for anything strange and curious as well a fascination for old articles and places. Journeys to such locations would suit you doubly because you love to travel and can gain a great deal from the trips that you make. Political, scientific and educational work might all be of interest to you and you would gain from a career in some new and exciting branch of science or technology.

Money-wise, you make gains through innovation as much as by concentration and it isn't unusual to find lunar Aquarians tackling more than one job at the same time. In love you are honest and kind.

MOON IN PISCES

This position assures you of a kind sympathetic nature, somewhat retiring at times but always taking account of others and doing your best to help them. As with all planets in Pisces there is bound to be some misfortune on the way through life. In particular relationships of a personal nature can be problematic and often through no real fault of your own. Inevitably though suffering brings a better understanding, both of yourself and of the world around you. With a fondness for travel you appreciate beauty and harmony wherever you encounter them and hate disorder and strife.

You are probably very fond of literature and could make a good writer or speaker yourself. The imagination that you possess can be readily translated into creativity and you might come across as an incurable romantic. Being naturally receptive your intuition is strong, in many cases verging on a mediumistic quality that sets you apart from the world. You might not be rich in hard cash terms and yet the gifts that you possess and display, when used properly, are worth more than gold.

THE ASTRAL DIARY

How the diagrams work

Through the *picture diagrams* in the Astral Diary I want to help you to plot your year. With them you can see where the positive and negative aspects will be found each month. To make the most of them all you have to do is remember where and when!

Let me show you how they work . . .

THE MONTH AT A GLANCE

Just as there are twelve separate Zodiac Signs, so Astrologers believe that each sign has twelve separate aspects to life. Each of the twelve segments relates to a different personal aspect. I number and list them all every month as a key so that their meanings are always clear.

The twelve major aspects of your life

Symbols above the box means 'positive'

Shading inside the box means 'ordinary'

| 1 | 2 | 3 | 4 | 5 | 6 | 7 | 8 | 9 | 10 | 11 | 12 |

Symbol below the box means 'negative'

I have designed this chart to show you how and when these twelve different aspects are being influenced throughout the year. When the number rests comfortably in its shaded box, nothing out of the ordinary is to be expected. However, when a box turns white, then you should expect influences to become active in this area of your life. Where the influence is positive I have raised a smiling sun above its number. Where it is a negative, I hang a little rain cloud beneath it.

YOUR ENERGY RHYTHM CHART

On the opposite page is a picture diagram in which I am linking your zodiac group to the rhythm of the moon. In doing this I have calculated when you will be gaining strength from its influence and equally when you may be weakened by it.

If you think of yourself as being like the tides of the ocean then you may understand how your own energies must rise and fall too. And if you understand how it works and when it is working, then you can better organise your activities to achieve more and get things done more easily.

YOUR ENERGY-RHYTHM CHART

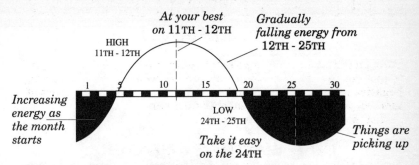

At your best on 11TH - 12TH

HIGH
11TH - 12TH

Gradually falling energy from 12TH - 25TH

1   5   10   15   20   25   30

Increasing energy as the month starts

LOW
24TH - 25TH

Take it easy on the 24TH

Things are picking up

MOVING PICTURE SCREEN
Measured every week

LOVE, LUCK, MONEY & VITALITY

I hope that the diagram below offers more than a little fun. It is very easy to use. The bars move across the scale to give you some idea of the strength of opportunities open to you in each of the four areas. If LOVE stands at plus 4, then get out and put yourself about, because in terms of romance, things should be going your way. When the bar moves backwards then the opportunities are weakening and when it enters the negative scale, then romance should not be at the top of your list.

Not a good week for money

← NEGATIVE TREND

Love at +4 promises a romantic week

POSITIVE TREND →

	-5	-4	-3	-2	-1		+1	+2	+3	+4	+5
LOVE											
MONEY											
LUCK											
VITALITY											

Below average for vitality

And your luck in general is good

And Finally:

am ....

pm .... 🔑

The two lines that are left blank in each daily entry of the Astral Diary are for your own personal use. You may find them ideal for keeping a check on birthdays or appointments, though it could be an idea to make notes from the astrological trends and diagrams a few weeks in advance. Some of the lines carry a key, as above. These days are important because they indicate the working of 'astrological cycles' in your life. The key readings show how best you can act, react or simply work within them for greater success.

1994
YOUR MONTH AT A GLANCE

The twelve numbered boxes represent the important areas in your life. The key to the numbers you will find beneath the panel. A Sun above the number indicates that opportunities are around. A Cloud below the number, that you should be a bit defensive. Nothing above or below and life will be pretty ordinary.

1	2	3	4	5	6	7	8	9	10	11	12

KEY

1 Strength of Personality	7 One to One Relationships
2 Personal Finance	8 Questioning, Thinking & Deciding
3 Useful Information Gathering	9 External Influences / Education
4 Domestic Affairs	10 Career Aspirations
5 Pleasure & Romance	11 Teamwork Activities
6 Effective Work & Health	12 Unconscious Impulses

OCTOBER HIGHS AND LOWS

Here, I show how the rhythm of the Moon will affect you this month. Like the tide, your energies and abilities will rise and fall with its pattern. When it is above the date line, go-for-it. When it is below the line you should be resting.

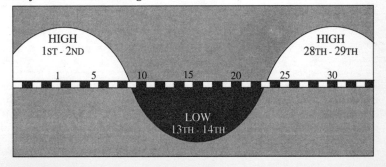

3 MONDAY
Moon Age Day 28 • Moon Sign Virgo

am ....

pm ....

With the Sun presently in your solar fourth house, look for a day of high energy and a busy pace to everyday routines. Life should be generally satisfying, and you have the ability to handle many different tasks simultaneously. The key to success at present lies in versatility, plus an added dose of cheerfulness.

4 TUESDAY
Moon Age Day 29 • Moon Sign Virgo

am ....

pm ....

Mars enters your solar first house and helps you to put thoughts of the past firmly where they belong. You should be conscious of the fact that you are preparing for a new phase of vigorous action and already your leadership qualities and the competitive edge to your nature may be beginning to show.

5 WEDNESDAY
Moon Age Day 0 • Moon Sign Libra

am ....

pm ....

You are in a playful and pleasing mood with others and what's more you should be less insensitive to their feelings than might sometimes be the case for Leo. Exciting prospects are on offer socially and you can meet a number of different types of individuals en route through life.

6 THURSDAY
Moon Age Day 1 • Moon Sign Libra

am ....

pm ....

The restless side of your spirit is stimulated today and you become especially impatient with authorities, or those types of people who appear to be holding you back. Feeling cramped by domestic matters, or perhaps the demands of your partner, you need to find space to be alone to think things out.

7 FRIDAY
Moon Age Day 2 • Moon Sign Scorpio

am ....

pm ....

A favourable association of Mercury and Saturn, presently in your chart, enables you to take a serious and responsible approach to obligations and marks a change in attitude from previous days. Others should be highly impressed by your common-sense attitude, and with only a little effort on your part.

8 SATURDAY
Moon Age Day 3 • Moon Sign Scorpio

am ....

pm ....

Despite the fact that you should have social and leisure time to spare today, distractions do occur. You probably prefer to remain committed to the needs of your partner in an emotional sense and need not venture too far in order to experience the kind of pleasure that appeals to you at present.

9 SUNDAY
Moon Age Day 4 • Moon Sign Sagittarius

am ....

pm ....

Mars in your solar first house brings a physical high and allows you to accomplish a great deal, despite the general restful qualities inherent in Sunday. If ever you came across a time for burning the candle at both ends, this is it. Be prepared later in the week to stand up for less confident types.

← NEGATIVE TREND   *POSITIVE TREND →*

-5	-4	-3	-2	-1		+1	+2	+3	+4	+5
					LOVE					
					MONEY					
					LUCK					
					VITALITY					

10 MONDAY   *Moon Age Day 5 • Moon Sign Sagittarius*

am ....

pm ....

Socially, if not professionally, you will be feeling at odds with others today, finding their basic viewpoints incompatible with your own. In reality, it would be best to agree to disagree. The same general trends occur with regard to your love life, though a better chance of a deep understanding is noticeable later.

11 TUESDAY   *Moon Age Day 6 • Moon Sign Capricorn*

am ....

pm ....

The encouragement of those around you, and particularly loved ones, may persuade you to take things more steadily. Your desire both to give and receive love are especially stimulated and you should be able to gain from exciting happenings in your vicinity, even if some of these come as genuine surprises.

12 WEDNESDAY   *Moon Age Day 7 • Moon Sign Capricorn*

am ....

pm ....

Avoid being too finicky about work plans, or general developments in your life. Any attempt to make things perfect today could fail and by so doing you will waste valuable time and slow down general progress. You are apt to be a bit blunt in conversation at present, and need to show a little patience.

13 THURSDAY   *Moon Age Day 8 • Moon Sign Aquarius*

am ....

pm ....

The lunar low brings a need for you to find time for yourself which probably is a compensation for hours devoted to the obligations and duties which have pressed in so hard over the last few days. Accepting the odd moods that predominate today is a natural part of life and you are able to plan well.

14 FRIDAY
Moon Age Day 9 • Moon Sign Aquarius

am ....

pm ....

If you start out today expecting blocks to general progress, you will deal with them that much better. It is important, despite the position of the Moon, to remain persistent and not to give in to a lethargic frame of mind. Not the best day to initiate ambitious schemes, but a better one for finishing off existing tasks.

15 SATURDAY
Moon Age Day 10 • Moon Sign Pisces

am ....

pm ....

The Moon moves away into your solar eighth house, bringing promising potential for limited financial speculation. Joint financial involvements look good and the close ties you feel to others bring a warm and secure feeling into your life. This might be a favourable period for making minor changes.

16 SUNDAY
Moon Age Day 11 • Moon Sign Pisces

am ....

pm ....

An adverse aspect to Neptune brings a need for freedom and the space to pursue your own objectives. Others may view your ideas as being slightly eccentric and certainly unpredictable. Once you have had the time to explain yourself however, all should be well. Keep a careful check on health matters.

← *NEGATIVE TREND*   *POSITIVE TREND* →

-5	-4	-3	-2	-1			+1	+2	+3	+4	+5
					LOVE						
					MONEY						
					LUCK						
					VITALITY						

17 MONDAY

Moon Age Day 12 • Moon Sign Pisces

am ....

pm ....

It is important to vary your lifestyle and routines as much as possible, because you may be in danger of getting into a rut. Pleasure trips, perhaps after work, may be the only tonic you require to lift your spirits, though even apparently random events, bring experiences that are out of the ordinary.

18 TUESDAY

Moon Age Day 13 • Moon Sign Aries

am ....

pm ....

Information on news that you have been expecting, regarding professional or personal projects, may fail to arrive. The present position of Mercury in your solar chart is responsible, and you will need to double check on appointments, or any kind of travel arrangement. As the day goes on, you become more pessimistic.

19 WEDNESDAY

Moon Age Day 14 • Moon Sign Aries

am ....

pm ....

For a number of reasons, you are reluctant to join in with the rest of the group socially today. Unlike the typically gregarious Leo, you remain in your own shell, but even this may not be an ill-wind, because it bring the opportunity to work carefully and diligently on long term plans.

20 THURSDAY

Moon Age Day 15 • Moon Sign Taurus

am ....

pm ....

A higher profile now comes along, and there is the possibility of you attracting romantic attention, even unintentionally. Not a good period for trying to mix business with pleasure, but when you are working hard, your efforts impress superiors and colleagues alike. Keep your eyes and ears open for professional opportunities.

21 FRIDAY

Moon Age Day 16 • Moon Sign Taurus

am ....

pm ....

The present position of Venus is inclined to encourage you to keep company with one special person at present, and not to behave in your usual gregarious manner. This is not a time for group activities, though family and domestic situations may be the direction you choose to turn in.

22 SATURDAY

Moon Age Day 17 • Moon Sign Taurus

am ....

pm ....

A day of apparently dramatic events, though the long term implications of these may prove to be less awe-inspiring. People close to you have strong points of view and since you are not about to back down yourself, confrontations could be the result. Somebody especially close to you could act as a diplomat.

23 SUNDAY

Moon Age Day 18 • Moon Sign Gemini

am ....

pm ....

The Sun enters your solar fourth house, bringing a new period of reward that will show itself, on and off, for the next month or so. Major benefits today come as a result of your partner and are associated with your home life in some way. Information about celebrations, or general domestic arrangements breaks the routine.

← NEGATIVE TREND								POSITIVE TREND →			
-5	-4	-3	-2	-1			+1	+2	+3	+4	+5
					LOVE						
					MONEY						
					LUCK						
					VITALITY						

24 MONDAY
Moon Age Day 19 • Moon Sign Gemini

am ....

pm ....

Mars is strong for you now, and you develop a better ability to handle pressure in a professional sense. Rivals or competitors mean little to you and you are forthright and frank in your communication with others. The Lion is now vigorous and healthy, but you may need to curb a little impatience.

25 TUESDAY
Moon Age Day 20 • Moon Sign Cancer

am ....

pm ....

Don't take on any more work commitments today than you know you can reasonably handle. There are plenty of jobs piling up and waiting to be done, both at work and at home. The general atmosphere of your life is relaxed and co-operative and you are able to show tremendous sympathy and generosity.

26 WEDNESDAY
Moon Age Day 21 • Moon Sign Cancer

am ....

pm ....

The present position of the Moon shows you to be in need of solitude with time to consider your own private thoughts and to resolve emotional issues which may be getting out of control. Don't let others talk you into involvements of which you are suspect, because there are some very unscrupulous characters around at present.

27 THURSDAY
Moon Age Day 22 • Moon Sign Cancer

am ....

pm ....

A good time to win friends and influence people, thanks to the lunar high which brightens your life no end today. Emotionally speaking, you feel strong and secure and in boisterous spirits, which are part of your nature today can be shared with others. Speculation is well highlighted and you might like to try a flutter.

28 FRIDAY

Moon Age Day 23 • Moon Sign Leo

am ....

pm ....

The best time this month to approach important people, or employers with regard to personal favours. You may be surprised by the responses coming in from the world at large, and you are in a position to push ahead with new or current plans of action. The most favourable results of all come when you remain cheerful.

29 SATURDAY

Moon Age Day 24 • Moon Sign Leo

am ....

pm ....

Actions taken today, and decisions made, turn out to be lucky in the extreme later on. Everyday routines are going quite smoothly, and most of your plans turn out as expected. Both colleagues, friends and relatives may have some surprising favours to offer. Be bold when chasing long-term objectives.

30 SUNDAY

Moon Age Day 25 • Moon Sign Virgo

am ....

pm ....

News is coming to light regarding professional or personal developments, which make your path ahead seem much clearer. Social gatherings and meetings of all kinds prove to be eventful and you may choose this time as being ideal to become involved in new hobbies or pastimes that you have barely even considered previously.

← NEGATIVE TREND							POSITIVE TREND →			
-5	-4	-3	-2	-1		+1	+2	+3	+4	+5
					LOVE					
					MONEY					
					LUCK					
					VITALITY					

31 MONDAY

Moon Age Day 26 • Moon Sign Virgo

am ....

pm ....

Minor adjustments are necessary to present work plans and practical matters bring distractions that cloud your judgement a little. Nevertheless, favourable progress is indicated for today, so much so, that you could tend to neglect the needs of loved ones by being too wrapped up in your own personal desires.

1 TUESDAY

Moon Age Day 27 • Moon Sign Libra

am ....

pm ....

Once again a routine sort of day, with little to set Tuesday apart as being anything exceptional. There is the vague possibility of diversifying into new interests and short journeys planned can be of interest. A rendezvous with someone you don't see very often can bring revealing news.

2 WEDNESDAY

Moon Age Day 28 • Moon Sign Libra

am ....

pm ....

Are other people really leading you up the garden-path today? Or is it just a frame of mind that you have got yourself into? Certainly it appears that those around you are unable to settle on any project, or to agree with even the most common point of view coming from your direction.

3 THURSDAY

Moon Age Day 0 • Moon Sign Scorpio

am ....

pm ....

The emphasis today is placed on matters close to your heart. You need to be around and with familiar faces and people, and show sentimental and nostalgic tendencies throughout the whole day. Loved ones prove to be reassuring and help to calm down minor worries that are not especially helpful today.

4 FRIDAY
Moon Age Day 1 • Moon Sign Scorpio

am ....

pm ....

Mars works hard in your solar first house, to reinforce a physical peak and bring a day of high activity. You may have a bee in your bonnet regarding a personal matter, and need to be careful when approaching or challenging others. However, those who know you the best will be reluctant to confront you.

5 SATURDAY
Moon Age Day 2 • Moon Sign Sagittarius

am ....

pm ....

With the start of the weekend, your love life especially proves to be pleasurable and rewarding. Others seem anxious to push you to the forefront and it is easier now to let go and be yourself than has been the case throughout the week. You should find the day mostly satisfying and full of possible romantic encounters.

6 SUNDAY
Moon Age Day 3 • Moon Sign Sagittarius

am ....

pm ....

A day to encounter others who can open up new possibilities in your life, both with regard to work and finances and also personally. You are sure to maintain current progress in routine matters and should avoid a tendency to drop everything in favour of new possibilities that look exciting and stimulating.

← NEGATIVE TREND   POSITIVE TREND →

-5	-4	-3	-2	-1			+1	+2	+3	+4	+5
					LOVE						
					MONEY						
					LUCK						
					VITALITY						

1994

YOUR MONTH AT A GLANCE

The twelve numbered boxes represent the important areas in your life. The key to the numbers you will find beneath the panel. A Sun above the number indicates that opportunities are around. A Cloud below the number, that you should be a bit defensive. Nothing above or below and life will be pretty ordinary.

1	2	3	4	5	6	7	8	9	10	11	12

KEY

1 Strength of Personality
2 Personal Finance
3 Useful Information Gathering
4 Domestic Affairs
5 Pleasure & Romance
6 Effective Work & Health

7 One to One Relationships
8 Questioning, Thinking & Deciding
9 External Influences / Education
10 Career Aspirations
11 Teamwork Activities
12 Unconscious Impulses

NOVEMBER HIGHS AND LOWS

Here, I show how the rhythm of the Moon will affect you this month. Like the tide, your energies and abilities will rise and fall with its pattern. When it is above the date line, go-for-it. When it is below the line you should be resting.

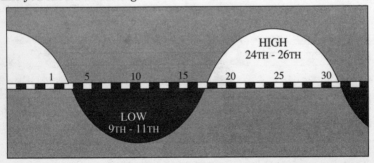

7 MONDAY
Moon Age Day 4 • Moon Sign Capricorn

am ....

pm ....

The emphasis, at the beginning of this week, is placed upon service and the sense of responsibility you feel towards those people close to you. You should be ready to lend a helping hand, not only at work, but also domestically and can be guaranteed to back worthy causes. Your own path through life is surefooted.

8 TUESDAY
Moon Age Day 5 • Moon Sign Capricorn

am ....

pm ....

Look out for minor disagreements at home, particularly since what you may consider to be trivial, from your point of view, others may take more seriously. It is all to easy at present to ruffle the feathers of loved ones and friends; a situation which is not aided by your tendency to be stubborn.

9 WEDNESDAY
Moon Age Day 6 • Moon Sign Aquarius

am ....

pm ....

The lunar low for the month leaves you feeling somewhat dispirited and more easily defeated than would generally be the case for Leo. Friends and colleagues alike are only too willing to point out that you are not up to par, but if you are sensible you will plod on regardless and do your best to take life in your stride.

10 THURSDAY
Moon Age Day 7 • Moon Sign Aquarius

am ....

pm ....

This is a day for delegating responsibility and almost automatically your partner, or work colleagues, will be happy to take necessary decisions. The general potential for success is not high and you may spend the majority of your time catching up on items that have become neglected within a busy schedule.

11 FRIDAY
Moon Age Day 8 • Moon Sign Aquarius

am ....

pm ....

Mercury moves into your solar fourth house, bringing a lull in professional matters. However, there is no fear of any disadvantage coming about as a result and at least you have the opportunity to spend some time in leisure pursuits and probably for taking up new hobbies. At home, life can become more hectic.

12 SATURDAY
Moon Age Day 9 • Moon Sign Pisces

am ....

pm ....

After a few quiet days, the pendulum swings and you discover an excellent time on the horizon. All joint efforts are well highlighted for the weekend and there may be some discussion regarding financial or property matters. Not a good period for confronting people about complicated situations of any sort.

13 SUNDAY
Moon Age Day 10 • Moon Sign Pisces

am ....

pm ....

Still generally exciting and eventful, life demands your attention in and around your home. There could not be a better time for throwing a party, or for having friends around simply for a chat. Look for the possibility of a reunion with friends from long ago, or the chance of communication with relatives far away.

14 MONDAY
Moon Age Day 11 • Moon Sign Aries

am ....

pm ....

A socially motivated week commences and the possibilities it offers lift your spirits. It isn't hard to achieve a meeting of minds with colleagues and for once the whole world seems to be on your wavelength. Friends could well be in need of your special brand of assistance, which you will be happy to supply.

15 TUESDAY
Moon Age Day 12 • Moon Sign Aries

am ....

pm ....

The pressures of your work and the obligations you feel to others will probably leave little time for socialising, though you should try to find an hour or two to pursue your personal desires and fancies. Watch out for life's tendency to make you into something that is quite alien to your basic nature.

16 WEDNESDAY
Moon Age Day 13 • Moon Sign Aries

am ....

pm ....

The favourable association of the Sun and Uranus means that even casual conversations can have far-reaching and positive implications. Opportunities come along to further your own ends financially, though special effort is required in all practical matters and not everything turns out as you would wish.

17 THURSDAY
Moon Age Day 14 • Moon Sign Taurus

am ....

pm ....

It is essential that you keep a cool head today and also that you stick with tried and tested methods of getting things done. There are many demands upon your generous nature and with requests coming in from all sides, a higher degree of patience is also called for. Resist the temptation to rush anything.

18 FRIDAY

Moon Age Day 15 • Moon Sign Taurus

am ....

pm ....

Dramatic or emotional encounters at home are possible, even though it could be your considered opinion that others are making far too much fuss about nothing. Despite this, the general feeling is positive and you remain cheerful. This is an excellent time for making changes domestically.

19 SATURDAY

Moon Age Day 16 • Moon Sign Gemini

am ....

pm ....

A busy social scene sets the weekend apart and you should be careful not to make commitments or promises that you cannot keep. Life throws up a broad spectrum of interests and there is a danger that you could spread yourself too thinly. Scattered energies at this time will achieve nothing.

20 SUNDAY

Moon Age Day 17 • Moon Sign Gemini

am ....

pm ....

Mars is strong in your solar first house, bringing a period that promises to be exciting with you at the forefront of events. Not everything that you do now appears to make sense to others and you are also inclined to see challenges in what amount to minor situations. Make certain that you explain yourself.

← NEGATIVE TREND								POSITIVE TREND →			
-5	-4	-3	-2	-1			+1	+2	+3	+4	+5
					LOVE						
					MONEY						
					LUCK						
					VITALITY						

21 MONDAY
Moon Age Day 18 • Moon Sign Gemini

am ....

pm ....

The past can mean a great deal to you at this time, and with the Moon in your solar twelfth house this is not the best time to commence new, important or complicated projects. Practical and emotional help is forthcoming from others, but probably not today. All aspects of planning do work well.

22 TUESDAY
Moon Age Day 19 • Moon Sign Cancer

am ....

pm ....

The Sun now enters your solar fifth house, bringing a month-long period of social and emotional fulfilment. Romantic developments show more strongly than of late, so that new and fulfilling relationships can commence at this time. The full power of your personality can be brought to bear on events.

23 WEDNESDAY
Moon Age Day 20 • Moon Sign Cancer

am ....

pm ....

The present position of Mercury makes the time excellent for mental work, particularly that undertaken behind the scenes. Grant yourself a little leisure time, during which you may choose to put your feet up with a good book. Communication with people at home is very important, and more so in a day or two.

24 THURSDAY
Moon Age Day 21 • Moon Sign Leo

am ....

pm ....

Physical and emotional strength comes your way courtesy of the lunar high. This could prove to be one of the luckiest days of the month, and is excellent for taking chances. You should be able to achieve your aims with much more ease than at other times. Good luck comes your way, almost on its own.

25 FRIDAY
Moon Age Day 22 • Moon Sign Leo

am ....

pm ....

The end of the working week finds you taking the initiative in almost everything. Unexpected favours come from the direction of others, whilst romantic proposals and kind words from friends give you plenty to smile about. Plan for the weekend now and be prepared to put your ideas into action at the appropriate time.

26 SATURDAY
Moon Age Day 23 • Moon Sign Leo

am ....

pm ....

Get your priorities right today because there is possible conflict between the needs to pursue personal desires and the fulfilment of obligations regarding others. Ensure that you don't leave friends in the lurch, and that you remain energetic and forward looking. Definitely a good day for shopping for that special bargain.

27 SUNDAY
Moon Age Day 24 • Moon Sign Virgo

am ....

pm ....

Once again, conflict exists in your mind between the need to let go and have fun, and life's requirement that you attend to serious issues, especially emotional relationships. Be careful not to take advantage of other people's feelings, or their money. Plan carefully now for changes that prove to be imperative at work later.

← NEGATIVE TREND							POSITIVE TREND →			
-5	-4	-3	-2	-1			+1	+2	+3	+4	+5
					LOVE					
					MONEY					
					LUCK					
					VITALITY					

28 MONDAY   *Moon Age Day 25 • Moon Sign Virgo*

am ....

pm ....

All meetings, appointments, travel arrangements, etc., carry
favourable trends at present. Dealings with other people show how
much you can influence those around you, though later in the day it
is possible that you will receive invitations from others which for one
reason or another you feel compelled to refuse.

29 TUESDAY   *Moon Age Day 26 • Moon Sign Libra*

am ....

pm ....

Hitches are inevitable in everyday routine events. You can be
distracted or diverted from an original plan of action, but will still
be open to new experiences. Today's events can prove to be
rewarding and even financially lucrative in the long run. A good
chat with a friend aleviates some minor worries.

30 WEDNESDAY   *Moon Age Day 27 • Moon Sign Libra*

am ....

pm ....

Exhibiting the lightest of light touches, especially in your love life,
you are a source of inspiration for those closest to you. It is true
that others may expect more commitment than you are willing, or
able, to offer and you should endeavour to resist being weighed
down by heavy emotional demands.

1 THURSDAY   *Moon Age Day 28 • Moon Sign Scorpio*

am ....

pm ....

A few home truths have to be faced today. It really is best to bring
things out into the open, even if to do so is a little uncomfortable at
first. Significant developments are possible later in the day on a
domestic front, and long-term family planning becomes imperative if
you are to succeed ultimately.

2 FRIDAY

Moon Age Day 29 • Moon Sign Scorpio

am ....

pm ....

An over-riding need for security and to find the roots of your life, contradicts your general nature today and may also make you reluctant to accept social invitations, or to venture too far from home. You need to deal with tricky domestic issues as soon as they arise and to take a long hard look at aspects of your life.

3 SATURDAY

Moon Age Day 0 • Moon Sign Sagittarius

am ....

pm ....

Typical Leo traits are in evidence today, which means that you are out there in the main stream of life, having fun and influencing others positively. Happy to seek the attention of friends, you can get the most out of the stimulating company that surrounds you. The most important fact is that you need an audience.

4 SUNDAY

Moon Age Day 1 • Moon Sign Sagittarius

am ....

pm ....

There is a slight limit to your sense of freedom today, probably as a result of relationship commitments, which press heavily upon you. To neglect those closest to you now could be to your ultimate disadvantage. Judgements or decision making are apt to be faulty, particularly with regard to money matters, so do take care.

← NEGATIVE TREND							POSITIVE TREND →			
-5	-4	-3	-2	-1		+1	+2	+3	+4	+5
					LOVE					
					MONEY					
					LUCK					
					VITALITY					

1994

YOUR MONTH AT A GLANCE

The twelve numbered boxes represent the important areas in your life. The key to the numbers you will find beneath the panel. A Sun above the number indicates that opportunities are around. A Cloud below the number, that you should be a bit defensive. Nothing above or below and life will be pretty ordinary.

1	2	3	4	5	6	7	8	9	10	11	12

KEY

1 Strength of Personality
2 Personal Finance
3 Useful Information Gathering
4 Domestic Affairs
5 Pleasure & Romance
6 Effective Work & Health

7 One to One Relationships
8 Questioning, Thinking & Deciding
9 External Influences / Education
10 Career Aspirations
11 Teamwork Activities
12 Unconscious Impulses

DECEMBER HIGHS AND LOWS

Here, I show how the rhythm of the Moon will affect you this month. Like the tide, your energies and abilities will rise and fall with its pattern. When it is above the date line, go-for-it. When it is below the line you should be resting.

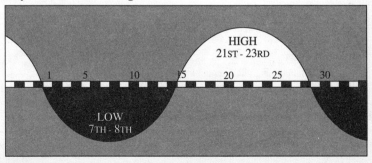

5 MONDAY
Moon Age Day 2 • Moon Sign Capricorn

am ....

pm ....

What a day for trying out new, or untested, methods of working. In fact, be wary of new or innovative ideas in a professional sense especially. It may be necessary to correct the mistakes of your co-workers, but don't allow frustrations to get the better of you, and especially not at home later in the day.

6 TUESDAY
Moon Age Day 3 • Moon Sign Capricorn

am ....

pm ....

Those around you have the upper-hand in work situations, or joint ventures, and the lunar low does nothing to cheer you up. It will probably be best to allow other people to have their way, especially as you could be feeling out of sorts. Avoid confrontations, unless you wish your ego to take a battering.

7 WEDNESDAY
Moon Age Day 4 • Moon Sign Aquarius

am ....

pm ....

Maintain a low profile and tie up any loose ends regarding duties or obligations. Not everyone in your vicinity proves to be reliable, even if it is through no fault of their own. Ensure that later in the day there is sufficient time both for leisure and relaxation.

8 THURSDAY
Moon Age Day 5 • Moon Sign Aquarius

am ....

pm ....

A period of generally hard work commences now, but the next couple of days are so productive you will be happy to put in the effort. Rewards achieved become more tangible and you should be actively seeking personal objectives. Don't be afraid to ask for what you want, since your powers of conversation are good.

9 FRIDAY

Moon Age Day 6 • Moon Sign Pisces

am ....

pm ....

Optimism rises as Jupiter enters your solar fifth house. This is especially the case with regard to all romantic possibilities and single Leos especially should be looking out new relationships at this time. You should be shining socially and feeling confident, no matter what company you are in.

10 SATURDAY

Moon Age Day 7 • Moon Sign Pisces

am ....

pm ....

Much drive is evident in your personal life and there are some signs that your hopes and ambitions are at last starting to come together. Personal plans are progressive and you are not about to let anyone stand in your way once your mind is made up. Friends seek you out for some impartial advice.

11 SUNDAY

Moon Age Day 8 • Moon Sign Aries

am ....

pm ....

A restless Leo puts in an appearance and you respond positively to a change of scene and some new faces in your vicinity. Horizons are broadened by travel and the emphasis is on leisure activities rather than on commitments to work or home. Make plans now for possible advancement at work in the week ahead.

← NEGATIVE TREND							POSITIVE TREND →			
-5	-4	-3	-2	-1			+1	+2	+3	+4	+5
					LOVE					
					MONEY					
					LUCK					
					VITALITY					

12 MONDAY

Moon Age Day 9 • Moon Sign Aries

am ....

pm ....

Too much concern with spending is not to be advised today, even though Christmas is just around the corner. Mars enters your solar second house, which does stimulate your desire nature and can make you a little more possessive than would usually be the case. In personal relationships, allow your partner some freedom.

13 TUESDAY

Moon Age Day 10 • Moon Sign Aries

am ....

pm ....

It is within your power to make today very special for someone; most likely your partner if you are an attached Leo. People in your vicinity need emotional reassurance and the affectionate qualities of your nature are stimulated. The openness you show to others is genuine and could lead to pleasant social encounters later.

14 WEDNESDAY

Moon Age Day 11 • Moon Sign Taurus

am ....

pm ....

Though headway is not hard to make professionally, specific plans and intentions may not be working out as you would wish. Extra effort is needed and you might turn in the direction of employers or superiors who seem to be holding you in high esteem at present. Make any requests now.

15 THURSDAY

Moon Age Day 12 • Moon Sign Taurus

am ....

pm ....

Others do their best to ferret information out of you, whilst you remain impassive and refuse to spill the beans. The secretive Lion does not put in an appearance very often, but you can see your silence as a means of removing obstacles from your path of progress. Tackle minor complications one at a time.

16 FRIDAY
Moon Age Day 13 • Moon Sign Gemini

am ....

pm ....

In what should be a fairly settled financial spell, current challenges
are dealt with easily. In the run up to Christmas, you are in
demand socially and are taking a very responsible attitude. Remain
sympathetic, even with people whose motives remain a mystery to
you. There are rewards later if you do.

17 SATURDAY
Moon Age Day 14 • Moon Sign Gemini

am ....

pm ....

Unless you are careful, extravagance carries the day, and there is a
danger of squandering money. The difficult association of Mars and
Jupiter is responsible and means that too large a percentage of your
resources could be spent on leisure pursuits. Nevertheless, exciting
times lie ahead before long.

18 SUNDAY
Moon Age Day 15 • Moon Sign Gemini

am ....

pm ....

Energies are somewhat limited, perhaps not surprising considering
the pace of your life over the past few days. Avoid being distracted
from the task in hand, even if it is only a routine job at home. Ideas
come and go at present, though most sensible Leos will be keeping
Christmas in mind and planning accordingly.

← *NEGATIVE TREND*   *POSITIVE TREND* →

-5	-4	-3	-2	-1		+1	+2	+3	+4	+5
					LOVE					
					MONEY					
					LUCK					
					VITALITY					

19 MONDAY

Moon Age Day 16 • Moon Sign Cancer

am ....

pm ....

Mental energy is good at the beginning of the working week, allowing you to get things done in half the usual time. Once again, avoid having too many professional involvements on the go at once, because there certainly won't be enough time to devote to all of them. Financial deals appear to be favourable.

20 TUESDAY

Moon Age Day 17 • Moon Sign Cancer

am ....

pm ....

Most Leos will now be looking for opportunities to improve the quality of their lives, probably through developments at work. Attention turns away from friends towards family members, with whom you find yourself in a giving mood. Sound practical assistance is at hand, as long as you are willing to accept it.

21 WEDNESDAY

Moon Age Day 18 • Moon Sign Leo

am ....

pm ....

The surge of energy coming in, courtesy of the lunar high, could not arrive at a better time. In the run up to the festivities, it is not difficult for you to handle several different tasks simultaneously, though assistance does come from loved ones and associates who do their best to make life easy.

22 THURSDAY

Moon Age Day 19 • Moon Sign Leo

am ....

pm ....

Life becomes exciting with friendships especially offering new incentives. Your greatest gift at present is your ability to attract the goodwill and generosity of others and as a result the day should be a fairly smooth one. Some limited speculation can be expected to pay dividends in a few days.

23 FRIDAY
Moon Age Day 20 • Moon Sign Leo

am ....

pm ....

The Sun enters your solar sixth house, placing the emphasis for the next month or so upon getting your personal circumstances in order. Minor details at work can be a problem if others are accusing you of being fussy; perhaps you are not doing much to help matters. For most Leos this is a vigorous spell.

24 SATURDAY
Moon Age Day 21 • Moon Sign Virgo

am ....

pm ....

A last financial fling before Christmas is not out of the question because your generosity is so well indicated. Be careful not to leave yourself short of money, and look out for good news concerning long term financial prospects. Your love life should be harmonious and once again life is easy going.

25 SUNDAY
Moon Age Day 22 • Moon Sign Virgo

am ....

pm ....

With the Moon in your solar third house, you may prefer to make social calls, rather than to invite others around. Minor cause for concern in family matters, means some time on your part smoothing things over. Socially speaking you will be happy to keep to a close circle of friends.

NEGATIVE TREND						POSITIVE TREND				
-5	-4	-3	-2	-1		+1	+2	+3	+4	+5
					LOVE					
					MONEY					
					LUCK					
					VITALITY					

26 MONDAY   *Moon Age Day 23 • Moon Sign Libra*

am ....

pm ....

It is not only prudent, but also useful, to keep on the good side of others today. Even casual remarks on your part could trigger off unexpected reactions. Some time spent with your partner may lead to discussions that are well overdue. You should be taking a more responsible attitude towards romance.

27 TUESDAY   *Moon Age Day 24 • Moon Sign Libra*

am ....

pm ....

There should be plenty today to keep you busy, involving pet projects and planning for the short rather than the long-term future. Routines are tedious, but do at least mean that things get done and since you are wearing your practical head today, nothing escapes your scrutiny. Leisure could suffer.

28 WEDNESDAY   *Moon Age Day 25 • Moon Sign Scorpio*

am ....

pm ....

It's people and situations close to home that warm your heart now. You can be quite relaxed, but should enjoy the general atmosphere in your vicinity. This is especially true since others are happy to relieve you of many responsibilities. Why not indulge yourself a little and do whatever really takes your fancy.

29 THURSDAY   *Moon Age Day 26 • Moon Sign Scorpio*

am ....

pm ....

As the end of the year approaches, you should be happy to clear up any loose ends regarding your personal life. Objects and situations which are down to others, could be cluttering your life or home at present, and you won't want them to hold you back in the future. Agreeable encounters attend your social life.

30 FRIDAY
Moon Age Day 27 • Moon Sign Sagittarius

am ....

pm ....

An association of Venus and Neptune is inclined to stimulate laziness and a reluctance on your part to carry out even routine duties, or obligations to others. Some Leos will take refuge in their imagination and will be looking out for the generous gestures coming from partners, relatives and close friends.

31 SATURDAY
Moon Age Day 28 • Moon Sign Sagittarius

am ....

pm ....

On the last day of 1994, you may find it difficult to relate to the standard behaviour of loved ones. All the same, the day is full of potentially agreeable and exciting situations. Don't work too hard, the emphasis now is upon leisure, with a special treat later in a romantic sense for many Lions.

1 SUNDAY
Moon Age Day 0 • Moon Sign Capricorn

am ....

pm ....

There is every incentive to put your best foot forward on the first day of the year, even though you may not get quite the early start that you may have planned. There are some good offers about, that is if you manage to keep your eyes open to look for them. Some effort on your part is quite vital now.

← NEGATIVE TREND						POSITIVE TREND →				
-5	-4	-3	-2	-1		+1	+2	+3	+4	+5
					LOVE					
					MONEY					
					LUCK					
					VITALITY					

1995

YOUR MONTH AT A GLANCE

The twelve numbered boxes represent the important areas in your life. The key to the numbers you will find beneath the panel. A Sun above the number indicates that opportunities are around. A Cloud below the number, that you should be a bit defensive. Nothing above or below and life will be pretty ordinary.

1	2	3	4	5	6	7	8	9	10	11	12

KEY

1 Strength of Personality
2 Personal Finance
3 Useful Information Gathering
4 Domestic Affairs
5 Pleasure & Romance
6 Effective Work & Health

7 One to One Relationships
8 Questioning, Thinking & Deciding
9 External Influences / Education
10 Career Aspirations
11 Teamwork Activities
12 Unconscious Impulses

JANUARY HIGHS AND LOWS

Here, I show how the rhythm of the Moon will affect you this month. Like the tide, your energies and abilities will rise and fall with its pattern. When it is above the date line, go-for-it. When it is below the line you should be resting.

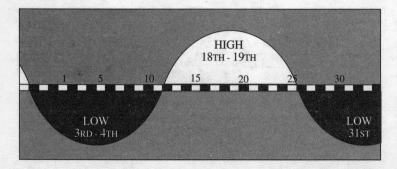

2 MONDAY

Moon Age Day 1 • Moon Sign Capricorn

am ....

pm ....

If you are back at work today you should find plenty to keep you occupied, whilst those of you who are still enjoying the holidays may want to catch up on the sort of jobs around the house that have waited during the Christmas period. Avoid family arguments, which you are unlikely to find yourself winning at present.

3 TUESDAY

Moon Age Day 2 • Moon Sign Aquarius

am ....

pm ....

Minor setbacks and let-downs are more or less an inevitable part of what you should expect today. The attitude of friends is rather difficult to fathom, mainly because they are not behaving in the way that you have come to expect. The more patience you can show, the less likely you are to run into difficulty.

4 WEDNESDAY

Moon Age Day 3 • Moon Sign Aquarius

am ....

pm ....

Beware of making rash decisions so early in the month. In reality, the moon is not in a good position for you at present and you would be far better advised to allow others to make some of the running for a change, whilst you sit back on the sidelines and watch the world go by. Confidences should not be broken.

5 THURSDAY

Moon Age Day 4 • Moon Sign Pisces

am ....

pm ....

All matters associated with work now take on a more leisurely feel, which is not to say that things are slow. On the contrary you are able to get all sorts done, though without having to push yourself all that hard. Creating the right atmosphere for the social possibilities that are in store for you could be especially important.

6 FRIDAY
Moon Age Day 5 • Moon Sign Pisces

am ....

pm ....

Tense situations need dealing with as and when they arise, and without you finding that there are other people trying to interfere with situations that are rightfully yours to deal with. An attitude problem on the part of a friend or a relative is something that you can take in your stride later in the day.

7 SATURDAY
Moon Age Day 6 • Moon Sign Pisces

am ....

pm ....

You tend to be rather too extravagant for your own good today, which although typical of your sign in some ways, is something that you should try and avoid if at all possible. Most people turn out to be reasonable in their attitude towards you, whilst social possibilities lift the quality of the day no end.

8 SUNDAY
Moon Age Day 7 • Moon Sign Aries

am ....

pm ....

Getting out and about ought to be on your agenda at the moment, even if it is not so immediately you rise this morning. Friends and family alike are inclined to demand your attention, which is something you need to get away from for a few hours at least. Comfort and security probably mean little to you right now.

← NEGATIVE TREND								POSITIVE TREND →		
-5	-4	-3	-2	-1		+1	+2	+3	+4	+5
					LOVE					
					MONEY					
					LUCK					
					VITALITY					

9 MONDAY
Moon Age Day 8 • Moon Sign Aries

am ....

pm ....

You should be very attentive to work details today and not allow the everyday pressures that build up around you to divert you from paths which you have freely chosen for yourself. Acting with determination, once you know that you have your facts right, you can make the world more or less what you want it to be.

10 TUESDAY
Moon Age Day 9 • Moon Sign Taurus

am ....

pm ....

Your usual Leonine need to be noticed is very much emphasised today and is one of the reasons why you are so willing to keep such a high profile when you are in any sort of public situation. Few people could fail to recognise what your potential is and all sorts of individuals come your way for help or advice.

11 WEDNESDAY
Moon Age Day 10 • Moon Sign Taurus

am ....

pm ....

The emphasis today is on pleasure pursuits and what you can do to improve the quality of the more social aspects of your life. Love and companionship are also very important, with a greater emphasis on the way that you are seen by the people you care about the most. Try not to be too demanding however.

12 THURSDAY
Moon Age Day 11 • Moon Sign Taurus

am ....

pm ....

It is in the social arena that you make the most headway at present, and the truth is that you can do yourself a deal of good financially too by mixing with the right people during the next few days. Confidence may not be quite as high as you would wish, though it certainly is increasing in the days ahead.

13 FRIDAY

Moon Age Day 12 • Moon Sign Gemini

am ....

pm ....

Most of the effort that you put into work today turns out to be favourable, even though it might not be directly as profitable as you might wish. A greater sense of determination allows you to push through all manner of changes at work, and this despite the fact that there are people around who want to hold you back.

14 SATURDAY

Moon Age Day 13 • Moon Sign Gemini

am ....

pm ....

With a new boost to romance on the horizon, you will want to make all you can out of relationships and what they have to offer you. Friends are very helpful and probably only too willing to put themselves out on your behalf. Confide in someone who is very dear to you if you feel that the time is right to do so.

15 SUNDAY

Moon Age Day 14 • Moon Sign Cancer

am ....

pm ....

An easy going sort of day, though perhaps not quite as exciting in one way or another as you might wish. A stitch in time now could save a great deal of work on the home front later on and also allows you to get cracking on something that has been important to you for quite some time.

NEGATIVE TREND							POSITIVE TREND				
-5	-4	-3	-2	-1			+1	+2	+3	+4	+5
					LOVE						
					MONEY						
					LUCK						
					VITALITY						

16 MONDAY
Moon Age Day 15 • Moon Sign Cancer

am ....

pm ....

This is a very good period for attracting the goodwill of others, and especially those who are in a position to do you some favour or other at work. There is little doubt that you are about to be offered more in the way of responsibility, though what you decide to do about the offer ends up being your choice in the end.

17 TUESDAY
Moon Age Day 16 • Moon Sign Cancer

am ....

pm ....

Probably the best part of the month for getting new schemes off the ground and for making the most of a more dynamic quality of nature. What you certainly cannot afford to do at present is to sit around and wait for life to make offers to you. The greater the effort you put in this week, the more you get from all situations.

18 WEDNESDAY
Moon Age Day 17 • Moon Sign Leo

am ....

pm ....

Good fortune follows you around, and never more so than during today. With more than your usual amount of good luck, you can afford to take the sort of chances that you would certainly have steered clear of even a few days ago. Continuity is important and you need to concentrate on any job that you have in hand.

19 THURSDAY
Moon Age Day 18 • Moon Sign Leo

am ....

pm ....

Minor financial gains are on the way, one or two of which you have not foreseen. Rules and regulations are inclined to get on your nerves at some stage and you are certainly not in the right frame of mind to listen to people who have no real point of view to put forward. Arguments could follow if you are provoked.

20 FRIDAY
Moon Age Day 19 • Moon Sign Virgo

am ....

pm ....

As the sun enters your solar seventh house, so you find that a new and a more rewarding period comes along, and especially so when it comes to the way that you are looking at personal relationships. Congratulations may be in order somewhere in the family, not that this prevents you from falling out with at least one family member.

21 SATURDAY
Moon Age Day 20 • Moon Sign Virgo

am ....

pm ....

This would be a very good time to discuss any problem that has been on your mind for quite a while. Those around you are attentive and now much more likely to see your point of view than they have done on a number of occasions in the recent past. For this reason, if no other, it would be useful to spill the beans.

22 SUNDAY
Moon Age Day 21 • Moon Sign Libra

am ....

pm ....

There may be some hidden anger lurking below the surface of your life and this tends to find its way to the forefront today, even in fairly casual conversations. A new and interesting interlude seems to be in store from a social point of view, which will at least take the edge of your tendency to be grumpy.

← *NEGATIVE TREND*   *POSITIVE TREND* →

-5	-4	-3	-2	-1			+1	+2	+3	+4	+5
					LOVE						
					MONEY						
					LUCK						
					VITALITY						

23 MONDAY   *Moon Age Day 22 • Moon Sign Libra*

am ....

pm ....

Loving relationships and social matters have a great part to play in your life at the moment and you do whatever you can to make those around you happy and contented. This may not always be easy in the midst of what is certainly a busy life, though you can find moments later in the day to show a more intimate feel.

24 TUESDAY   *Moon Age Day 23 • Moon Sign Scorpio*

am ....

pm ....

There are compliments coming in from a number of different directions, though one especially that means a great deal to you. It might be related to the more practical aspects of your life or could perhaps be associated with your need for greater stability at home. Whatever the reason, pin your ears back and enjoy the experience.

25 WEDNESDAY   *Moon Age Day 24 • Moon Sign Scorpio*

am ....

pm ....

More emotional reassurance is now necessary, which is one of the reasons why you are so willing to stay around those who have your best interest at heart and who will tell you things you really want to know. It isn't really like you to be in this frame of mind and fortunately is not a situation that will last very long.

26 THURSDAY   *Moon Age Day 25 • Moon Sign Scorpio*

am ....

pm ....

Social encounters and functions of all sorts tend not to live up to your expectations of them, which is why it would be best in most cases to simply wait and see what happens. The balanced your view, the better you feel about things in general, though achieving such a state of mind is not at all easy at present.

27 FRIDAY

Moon Age Day 26 • Moon Sign Sagittarius

am ....

pm ....

The more competitive edge returns to your nature and you will want
to be up there with the winners where life in general is concerned.
Today is not a time for hiding your light under a bushel of any sort
and you can get the most out of situations simply by being in the
right place at the right time.

28 SATURDAY

Moon Age Day 27 • Moon Sign Sagittarius

am ....

pm ....

You are prepared to do whatever it takes to make others like you,
and with this regard might show a tendency to go just a little too far.
Return to a simpler way of looking at most situations if it proves
possible for you to do so, or else you could find yourself in a position
where you fail to see the wood for the trees.

29 SUNDAY

Moon Age Day 28 • Moon Sign Capricorn

am ....

pm ....

Oversights or mistakes that you made in the past now come back to
dog your footsteps. In a general sense you are in a good frame of
mind and will be anxious to make all you can out of the offers that
the day brings with it. Concern for younger or less motivated family
members is inclined to get in your way at some stage.

NEGATIVE TREND						POSITIVE TREND				
-5	-4	-3	-2	-1		+1	+2	+3	+4	+5
LOVE										
MONEY										
LUCK										
VITALITY										

30 MONDAY
Moon Age Day 2 9 • Moon Sign Capricorn

am ....

pm ....

Energy and enthusiasm seems to winding down a little, which might appear to be something of a bind at the start of a new working week. In reality, this phase allows you the chance to stand back and watch for a change, something you are not usually inclined to do. This allows for a far better over-view of life as a whole.

31 TUESDAY
Moon Age Day 0 • Moon Sign Aquarius

am ....

pm ....

Those closest to you in a professional sense appear to be making more progress than you are, a situation that is not likely to please you all that much. Someone could have some advice that would help you to catch up, though in the main you are more inclined to please yourself and will not want to listen more than you have to.

1 WEDNESDAY
Moon Age Day 1 • Moon Sign Aquarius

am ....

pm ....

You tend to go it alone today, even when you know that there are those around who have excellent ideas and the ability to put them into practice. It is possible that you do yourself very few favours by being unwilling to cooperate at all, particularly if the reason is that you are envious of someone who has your best interests at heart.

2 THURSDAY
Moon Age Day 2 • Moon Sign Pisces

am ....

pm ....

Sudden, though minor, disruptions to your personal and social life simply have to be taken in your stride today. There is no point in reacting violently to any situation that you know would be best dealt with by simply remaining calm and waiting to see what happens. A new and interesting financial period begins.

3 FRIDAY

Moon Age Day 3 • Moon Sign Pisces

am ....

pm ....

Unexpected social invitations come along at this time and allow you the freedom to get away from some of the routines that have dogged you for a while. A great period opens for communicating your ideas to others and for getting what you want out of life in a more materialistic sense. Make the most of rapidly changing times.

4 SATURDAY

Moon Age Day 4 • Moon Sign Aries

am ....

pm ....

Work issues go more smoothly, in the case of some of you probably because you do not actually go to work on a Saturday. At home you are anxious to show just how interesting you can be and will want to catch up on gossip within the family that you have not had access to for quite a time. Show a loved one how much you care.

5 SUNDAY

Moon Age Day 5 • Moon Sign Aries

am ....

pm ....

There is some sort of conflict between personal and social matters, so much so that you are really stuck between the devil and the deep blue sea. It ought to be possible to find ways of reconciling the various needs within you, though possibly not before you have thought things through in a careful and detached way.

← *NEGATIVE TREND*							*POSITIVE TREND* →			
-5	-4	-3	-2	-1		+1	+2	+3	+4	+5
					LOVE					
					MONEY					
					LUCK					
					VITALITY					

1995

YOUR MONTH AT A GLANCE

The twelve numbered boxes represent the important areas in your life. The key to the numbers you will find beneath the panel. A Sun above the number indicates that opportunities are around. A Cloud below the number, that you should be a bit defensive. Nothing above or below and life will be pretty ordinary.

1	2	3	4	5	6	7	8	9	10	11	12

KEY

1 Strength of Personality
2 Personal Finance
3 Useful Information Gathering
4 Domestic Affairs
5 Pleasure & Romance
6 Effective Work & Health

7 One to One Relationships
8 Questioning, Thinking & Deciding
9 External Influences / Education
10 Career Aspirations
11 Teamwork Activities
12 Unconscious Impulses

FEBRUARY HIGHS AND LOWS

Here, I show how the rhythm of the Moon will affect you this month. Like the tide, your energies and abilities will rise and fall with its pattern. When it is above the date line, go-for-it. When it is below the line you should be resting.

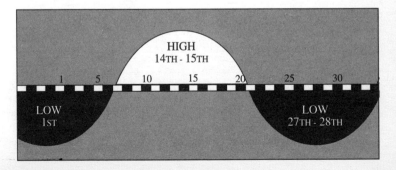

6 MONDAY

Moon Age Day 6 • Moon Sign Aries

am ....

pm ....

Professional and career commitments appear to be receiving most of your attention as the new working week gets underway. There are one or two false starts possible at this time, though these should not turn your mind away from genuinely important matters that prove to be the building blocks of success at some later date.

7 TUESDAY

Moon Age Day 7 • Moon Sign Taurus

am ....

pm ....

Friends and colleagues prove to be very talkative today, which should suit you down to the ground since you are in a very similar frame of mind yourself. Do all that you can to show others how much you care, both at work and at home. Catching up on jobs from the past is inclined to take up much of your time.

8 WEDNESDAY

Moon Age Day 8 • Moon Sign Taurus

am ....

pm ....

One-to-one relationships and friendships in general appear to be of supreme importance at some stage today. There may not be as much time as you would wish for pleasing yourself, or for doing the sort of things that you know to be of great interest. Still, you can pace yourself and achieve more from your efforts.

9 THURSDAY

Moon Age Day 9 • Moon Sign Gemini

am ....

pm ....

You may be spreading yourself more thinly than is strictly necessary, mainly because you see it as being your duty to be involved in almost anything that is going on in your vicinity. Creating a happy atmosphere at home will take up a proportion of your time, though you cannot turn away from social requirements.

10 FRIDAY
Moon Age Day 10 • Moon Sign Gemini

am ....

pm ....

Helpful and friendly assistance comes from a number of different directions, and helps you to look at your own day in a slightly different way than might otherwise be the case. Your ears are definitely open to the sort of advice that you know to be extremely useful and you put yourself out for almost anyone.

11 SATURDAY
Moon Age Day 11 • Moon Sign Gemini

am ....

pm ....

Lack of personal influence over others could be something that you have to deal with today, though fortunately not for very long. It's true that you are not being listened to as much as you would wish and you need to be aware that much of what you have to say has a subconscious effect that shows out later.

12 SUNDAY
Moon Age Day 12 • Moon Sign Cancer

am ....

pm ....

Tempers can be rather stronger than they should be, and that means having to count to ten before you allow yourself to react too harshly to almost any situation. Confidence is not as high as might be the case, though with a Sunday in view you might have decided that work is for the birds in any case.

← NEGATIVE TREND						POSITIVE TREND →				
-5	-4	-3	-2	-1		+1	+2	+3	+4	+5
					LOVE					
					MONEY					
					LUCK					
					VITALITY					

13 MONDAY
Moon Age Day 13 • Moon Sign Cancer

am ....

pm ....

This is the best time for making any sort of speedy progress and you will be not at all happy to discover that circumstances are holding you back in any way. Seeking what you want from life is a process that can take days, weeks or months, though there is little doubt that at least part of the effort is put in now.

14 TUESDAY
Moon Age Day 14 • Moon Sign Leo

am ....

pm ....

A mental peak comes along, during which your mind is razor sharp and you find yourself able to do whatever it takes to get others on your side. Intuition is also much stronger than you might anticipate and you have reserves of strength and endurance which might surprise even you. Friends can be of great assistance.

15 WEDNESDAY
Moon Age Day 15 • Moon Sign Leo

am ....

pm ....

Your judgement is as sound as can be and there are situations around that really respond to the sort of touch which only you can offer to a situation. Congratulations are the order of the day somewhere in your circle, with options for a host of new ideas to be put into action. Create a happy atmosphere at home.

16 THURSDAY
Moon Age Day 16 • Moon Sign Virgo

am ....

pm ....

This is a hard working and productive day, but perhaps not the most entertaining interlude that you are likely to encounter this week. Considering the needs and wants of others is something that is really important to you at present and you do all that you can to make life interesting and entertaining for those you love.

17 FRIDAY
Moon Age Day 17 • Moon Sign Virgo

am ....

pm ....

The way that your partner, or possibly some other family member, is behaving, can be mystifying to say the least. It is possible that there are facts that you are not party to and so a few suitable questions could prove to be in order. If certain aspects of life look precarious, deal with them head-on.

18 SATURDAY
Moon Age Day 18 • Moon Sign Virgo

am ....

pm ....

Meetings of any sort, together with travel and the ability to move about generally, are all especially important at this time. Confronting situations that you do not care for the look of will be important to you and there are some situations to be dealt with that you would definitely rather leave until a later date.

19 SUNDAY
Moon Age Day 19 • Moon Sign Libra

am ....

pm ....

A new period for change, diversity and revival now comes along. All in all this is a time for taking life by the scruff of the neck and for making it do the things that you really want it to. If you wait to be asked, regarding almost any situation, it is possible that you will find yourself left out in the cold.

← NEGATIVE TREND							POSITIVE TREND →			
-5	-4	-3	-2	-1		+1	+2	+3	+4	+5
					LOVE					
					MONEY					
					LUCK					
					VITALITY					

20 MONDAY
Moon Age Day 20 • Moon Sign Libra

am ....

pm ....

Family and domestic squabbles are clearly something that you would want to avoid if at all possible right now. Being the sort of person that you are, it is difficult for you to walk away from such situations and biting your lip never did come very easily. In the end you will be happy enough that you did not take part.

21 TUESDAY
Moon Age Day 21 • Moon Sign Scopio

am ....

pm ....

Sometimes even the best laid plans can go wrong, and especially so in your case right now. Confronting situations that you do not care for the look of is something that you simply have to take in your stride and in the meantime you can do much to improve your lot, even if it has to be done from the sidelines.

22 WEDNESDAY
Moon Age Day 22 • Moon Sign Scopio

am ....

pm ....

Romance and all leisure pursuits now have a bigger part to play in your life and you could be looking longingly towards a potential relationship that you know to be especially good. The atmosphere around your home should be very happy and you have plenty of reason to fuel more secure now that of late.

23 THURSDAY
Moon Age Day 23 • Moon Sign Sagittarius

am ....

pm ....

Any important deals of negotiations are likely to be undertaken today, that is if you have any choice in the matter. This would turn out to be a very good thing, since you are in the right frame of mind to put your point of view with courage and some force. This can be achieved without treading on the toes of others.

24 FRIDAY
Moon Age Day 24 • Moon Sign Sagittarius

am ....

pm ....

Don't take on more than you really know that you can handle, at least not for the moment. You should take the feelings of your partner into account whenever possible and indulge in the sort of discussions that you know to be sensible and serve a purpose in the longer term. Routines can prove to be a real drag.

25 SATURDAY
Moon Age Day 25 • Moon Sign Capricorn

am ....

pm ....

All sorts of financial pressures are placed upon you at the moment, though in reality you may not be looking at things as sensibly as should be the case. There is a strained atmosphere about at home, even though you may not be responsible for it. Creating space to be yourself is not at all easy right now.

26 SUNDAY
Moon Age Day 26 • Moon Sign Capricorn

am ....

pm ....

You can overestimate your own importance, a factor which always has to be guarded against with your sign. All the same you are capable of a great deal just at present and will want to do all that you can to get your message across intact, no matter what it might be. Confirming suspicions from the past is also important.

← *NEGATIVE TREND*   *POSITIVE TREND* →

-5	-4	-3	-2	-1		+1	+2	+3	+4	+5
					LOVE					
					MONEY					
					LUCK					
					VITALITY					

27 MONDAY

Moon Age Day 27 • Moon Sign Aquarius

am ....

pm ....

You can run out of steam all too easily at the start of this week and so may want to pace yourself a little. The more slowly and steadily you embark on any sort of job, the better is your ability to see it through to a sensible conclusion. Creating a good atmosphere at home is now essential to your wellbeing.

28 TUESDAY

Moon Age Day 28 • Moon Sign Aquarius

am ....

pm ....

Let your partner or an associate handle matters in the best way that they know how, whilst you get on with matters that are much more up your street. You don't really achieve very much by stepping on the toes of others are present and may only serve to make matters much worse than they would otherwise be.

1 WEDNESDAY

Moon Age Day 29 • Moon Sign Pisces

am ....

pm ....

Conflict can come like a bolt from the blue and if you do not want to find yourself involved in some sort of argument that can do you no good whatsoever, this is the time to be on your guard. Standing around and waiting for things to occur my not be as useful as looking at situations in advance of their happening.

2 THURSDAY

Moon Age Day 0 • Moon Sign Pisces

am ....

pm ....

A much lighter and more carefree attitude is now possible, thanks to the general influence of those people who have a vested interest in making you happy. Taking the line of least resistance at work could be a real path to successes, mainly because you have been so willing to put in the necessary effort earlier.

3 FRIDAY
Moon Age Day 1 • Moon Sign Aries

am ....

pm ....

Opt for a change of scene whenever it proves possible and see what can be done to ring the changes at work before the end of the week. What you really do not care for at the moment are the sort of routines that you know to be of little or no use to you and the last thing that you would want is to be tied down by them.

4 SATURDAY
Moon Age Day 2 • Moon Sign Aries

am ....

pm ....

Improvements to personal circumstances show an easy and carefree sort of weekend in prospect. Of course not everyone looks at life in quite the way that you do, a fact that you will have to deal with at some stage before the weekend is out. Other than this fact, life should be steady, interesting and eventful.

5 SUNDAY
Moon Age Day 3 • Moon Sign Aries

am ....

pm ....

There is no doubting that your spirits are high or that you can turn most circumstances round to your own way of thinking. Attitudes are variable and you have some niggles at the back of your mind that will have to be dealt with directly in the near future. Keep to tried and tested paths when dealing with family matters.

← *NEGATIVE TREND*   *POSITIVE TREND* →

-5	-4	-3	-2	-1			+1	+2	+3	+4	+5
					LOVE						
					MONEY						
					LUCK						
					VITALITY						

1995

YOUR MONTH AT A GLANCE

The twelve numbered boxes represent the important areas in your life. The key to the numbers you will find beneath the panel. A Sun above the number indicates that opportunities are around. A Cloud below the number, that you should be a bit defensive. Nothing above or below and life will be pretty ordinary.

1	2	3	4	5	6	7	8	9	10	11	12

Suns above 1, 2, 7. Clouds below 2, 10.

KEY

1 Strength of Personality	7 One to One Relationships
2 Personal Finance	8 Questioning, Thinking & Deciding
3 Useful Information Gathering	9 External Influences / Education
4 Domestic Affairs	10 Career Aspirations
5 Pleasure & Romance	11 Teamwork Activities
6 Effective Work & Health	12 Unconscious Impulses

MARCH HIGHS AND LOWS

Here, I show how the rhythm of the Moon will affect you this month. Like the tide, your energies and abilities will rise and fall with its pattern. When it is above the date line, go-for-it. When it is below the line you should be resting.

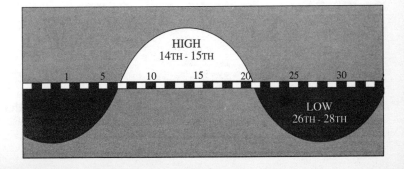

HIGH
14TH - 15TH

LOW
26TH - 28TH

6 MONDAY
Moon Age Day 4 • Moon Sign Taurus

am ....

pm ....

You may be in a more powerful position than you think today and will be doing all that you can to make the day go with a swing. With plenty of enthusiasm at your disposal, plus the ability to bring others round to your point of view, there is no reason at all why you should not find the day to be very eventful.

7 TUESDAY
Moon Age Day 5 • Moon Sign Taurus

am ....

pm ....

Avoid clashes with others that you know to be of no real use. You will not get anywhere by arguing about facts and figures that you cannot back up with something more substantial than fine words. Confidence to do the right thing is certainly not lacking, though might appear to be so at first.

8 WEDNESDAY
Moon Age Day 6 • Moon Sign Gemini

am ....

pm ....

The degree of friendship that certain other people show you today is so strong that you will be amazed at its power. Conflict is something that does not appear to enter your life at present and you can be fairly certain of an interesting and eventful sort of day. Not everyone has your best interests at heart however.

9 THURSDAY
Moon Age Day 7 • Moon Sign Gemini

am ....

pm ....

There is a boost coming along to your personal confidence, thanks to the intervention in your life of people who have played an important part in your life for some time. Be bold when you are dealing with work situations and do not allow yourself to be tied down to routines that you do not care for the look of.

10 FRIDAY   *Moon Age Day 8 • Moon Sign Gemini*

am ....

pm ....

Though most social affairs do go well enough there are certain people around who you simply do not care for the look of. All you can really do is to look at the matter sensibly and work out how best to deal with each situation as and when it arises. A very satisfying period if you decide to opt for anything creative.

11 SATURDAY   *Moon Age Day 9 • Moon Sign Cancer*

am ....

pm ....

This is an excellent time for all one-to-one relationships, and for doing things for family members and friends alike. A careful look at your finances could lead you to believe that things are more settled and stable than you might have previously thought. Confine yourself to interests that are really close to your heart.

12 SUNDAY   *Moon Age Day 10 • Moon Sign Cancer*

am ....

pm ....

A personal or emotional matter is something that you want to come to terms with as soon as you are able today. Act only when you have thought things through as carefully as you can and do not allow yourself to be tied down to any sort of routine that goes against the grain. Personalities abound in your life at the present time and continue to do so for some time ahead.

← *NEGATIVE TREND*   *POSITIVE TREND* →

-5	-4	-3	-2	-1		+1	+2	+3	+4	+5
					LOVE					
					MONEY					
					LUCK					
					VITALITY					

13 MONDAY
Moon Age Day 11 • Moon Sign Leo

am ....

pm ....

You can easily bring others round to your point of view right now, a fact that means they are much more likely to be sensible in the way they put themselves out to help you henceforth. Keep an open mind about changes that are taking place at work and do what you can to support people who are not as strong as you are.

14 TUESDAY
Moon Age Day 12 • Moon Sign Leo

am ....

pm ....

Along comes an emotional peak, and brings with it all the incentives that you need to get on in life in almost any way that takes your fancy. You are cool, sensible and wise, and possess all the qualities to act at your Leo best. Confirm all appointments well in advance and don't be distracted by details.

15 WEDNESDAY
Moon Age Day 13 • Moon Sign Leo

am ....

pm ....

An excellent period for solving problems of almost any sort, and for coming to terms with situations that have given you more than a little trouble in the past. Your mind is clear and you should also have much energy at your disposal. Conversations are interesting and feed you with all sorts of possibilities.

16 THURSDAY
Moon Age Day 14 • Moon Sign Virgo

am ....

pm ....

Working along may be preferable to doing things in the company of others. It is not really like you to shun company, though for the moment you are best left to your own devices. A creative period comes around again and it could be that you find yourself on the receiving end of offers you would find difficult to refuse.

17 FRIDAY

Moon Age Day 15 • Moon Sign Virgo

am ....

pm ....

Getting out and about proves to be very rewarding at the end of the working week and offers you the sort of incentives that you have been looking for for a while. Concern for the under-dog seems to be part of your thinking today but you can only stick up for others as much as they are willing to allow you to do.

18 SATURDAY

Moon Age Day 16 • Moon Sign Libra

am ....

pm ....

A physical peak now arrives, where any lack of energy is suddenly replaced by the all the incentives you could possibly need. An occasional lapse into your own mind is no bad thing, and at least affords you the chance to look at life more realistically than has sometimes proved to be the case earlier in the month.

19 SUNDAY

Moon Age Day 17 • Moon Sign Libra

am ....

pm ....

Enjoying a few quiet hours on your own, you now find that you have plenty to keep you occupied, albeit in a more quiet and contemplative way. There is less scope than you would have wished to make the sort of progress that you know to be essential to your life as a whole, though things are only on a temporary hold.

← *NEGATIVE TREND*   *POSITIVE TREND* →

-5	-4	-3	-2	-1			+1	+2	+3	+4	+5
				▨	LOVE						
					MONEY		▨	▨			
					LUCK		▨	▨			
				▨	VITALITY						

20 MONDAY

Moon Age Day 18 • Moon Sign Scorpio

am ....

pm ....

New love could be arriving on the scene for single Leo people, as a direct contrast to the less positive situations of the recent past. Conflict, either in the family or further afield, should be avoided if at all possible in favour of seeing the point of view that others are trying so hard to put forward now.

21 TUESDAY

Moon Age Day 19 • Moon Sign Scorpio

am ....

pm ....

Life should become generally more interesting than it seems to have been for quite some time, and offers you the sort of incentives that find you able to look and plan well ahead. Good things are there for the taking at present, and all that really matters is your ability to make the best of what is on offer.

22 WEDNESDAY

Moon Age Day 20 • Moon Sign Sagittarius

am ....

pm ....

Romantic interests keep you excited and on the ball today. Energy levels are certainly not low and there is time to do almost anything that really takes your fancy. Comfort and security, although at the back of your mind, are not really all that important to you at present. Keep an open mind about relatives.

23 THURSDAY

Moon Age Day 21 • Moon Sign Sagittarius

am ....

pm ....

There may be some difficulties involved in the natural relationships that are not usually any sort of a problem to you at all. Creating the right impression to show others how well you are able to cope with life is something that you take in your stride today, and you have the incentives to look far ahead.

24 FRIDAY

Moon Age Day 22 • Moon Sign Capricorn

am ....

pm ....

Social and romantic issues are once again on your mind, allowing you to focus on situations that have been paramount in your thinking for some time, even if they have been pushed into the background. Resourceful and quite able to see what other people are getting at, your very ability to cooperate is your best friend today.

25 SATURDAY

Moon Age Day 23 • Moon Sign Capricorn

am ....

pm ....

You may be too concerned with certain practical aspects of life, some of which you cannot put right at the weekend in any case. Be as adventurous as you like once you are away from your own front door and don't allow the pressure of routines to get in your way when it comes to doing what is important to you personally.

26 SUNDAY

Moon Age Day 24 • Moon Sign Aquarius

am ....

pm ....

Energy and enthusiasm both take a nose-dive today, so you should not expect to get through quite as much as might often be the case. Creating yourself a small cocoon in which you can rest and relax is something that may be of much greater importance to you right now than would usually be the case. Not everyone understands your needs.

← NEGATIVE TREND						*POSITIVE TREND →*				
-5	-4	-3	-2	-1		+1	+2	+3	+4	+5
			▓		LOVE					
					MONEY	▓				
				▓	LUCK	▓				
			▓		VITALITY					

27 MONDAY
Moon Age Day 25 • Moon Sign Aquarius

am ....

pm ....

There may be snags and drawbacks to be dealt with at this time, some of which would be best dealt with by others. You cannot do yourself any harm at all by being willing to allow friends to take some of the strain. What you certainly do not need right now is to be reminded of how many responsibilities there are.

28 TUESDAY
Moon Age Day 26 • Moon Sign Aquarius

am ....

pm ....

This is an excellent period for close relationships of any sort, and particularly so where the attachment may be of a romantic nature. Despite possible pitfalls people are willing to talk to you in a sensible way and can offer the sort of incentives that may have been missing from your life for some time past.

29 WEDNESDAY
Moon Age Day 27 • Moon Sign Pisces

am ....

pm ....

Though assistance is offered by others, it probably is not being accepted by you. You show a great desire at the moment to go it alone and to be unwilling to put yourself out for situations that you genuinely do not care for the look of. Fatigue can be fought off, though it may well catch up with you at a later date.

30 THURSDAY
Moon Age Day 28 • Moon Sign Pisces

am ....

pm ....

Social occasions tend to be rather more interesting than you might imagine at first. The company of those people who you care about the most is something that you cannot deny yourself, and nor should you. Confusion of any sort at work can soon be sorted out if you are only willing to listen to an alternative point of view.

31 FRIDAY

Moon Age Day 0 • Moon Sign Aries

am ....

pm ....

Actions which are brought on by impatience are the ones that you will want to deal with as soon as you can today. The situation is hardly likely to be brought about by you personally and may well have more to do with the way that others are behaving. Your capacity for work knows no bounds at the end of this working week.

1 SATURDAY

Moon Age Day 1 • Moon Sign Aries

am ....

pm ....

There may be sudden disruptions to your schedules and routines, which although not bothering you all that much can be real drag when seen from the point of perspective of those around you. New social contacts are on the way and you may want to have a hand in setting up outings or adventures for later in the month.

2 SUNDAY

Moon Age Day 2 • Moon Sign Taurus

am ....

pm ....

What an excellent time this would be for travel, or for deciding that you want a genuine and long-lasting change of scene. Pursuits which require your undivided attention might be rather difficult to take on however, partly because you are just not in the right frame of mind to concentrate on anything exclusively.

← *NEGATIVE TREND*   *POSITIVE TREND* →

-5	-4	-3	-2	-1			+1	+2	+3	+4	+5
					LOVE						
					MONEY						
					LUCK						
					VITALITY						

APRIL

1995

YOUR MONTH AT A GLANCE

The twelve numbered boxes represent the important areas in your life.
The key to the numbers you will find beneath the panel. A Sun above
the number indicates that opportunities are around. A Cloud below
the number, that you should be a bit defensive. Nothing above or
below and life will be pretty ordinary.

		☀				☀	☀				
1	2	3	4	5	6	7	8	9	10	11	12
			☁						☁		

KEY

1 Strength of Personality

2 Personal Finance

3 Useful Information Gathering

4 Domestic Affairs

5 Pleasure & Romance

6 Effective Work & Health

7 One to One Relationships

8 Questioning, Thinking & Deciding

9 External Influences / Education

10 Career Aspirations

11 Teamwork Activities

12 Unconscious Impulses

APRIL HIGHS AND LOWS

Here, I show how the rhythm of the Moon will affect you this month.
Like the tide, your energies and abilities will rise and fall with its pattern. When it is above the date line, go-for-it. When it is below the
line you should be resting.

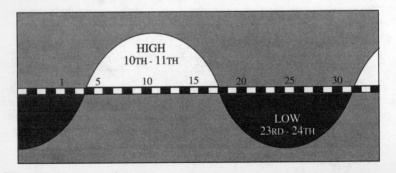

HIGH
10TH - 11TH

LOW
23RD - 24TH

3 MONDAY
Moon Age Day 3 • Moon Sign Taurus

am ....

pm ....

Although this should be generally a high-profile sort of day it appears that you need to approval of others before you can really get yourself into gear concerning new projects or schemes of almost any sort. Not everyone has your best interests at heart and so more than a little caution would be adviseable.

4 TUESDAY
Moon Age Day 4 • Moon Sign Taurus

am ....

pm ....

Your generous nature is apparent to almost everyone you come across today, which is why others are so willing now to put themselves out on your behalf. Act with determination at work and don't allow your own schemes to be either stolen or in some way watered down by people who really should know better.

5 WEDNESDAY
Moon Age Day 5 • Moon Sign Gemini

am ....

pm ....

If you are out and about today, you can make the most of the period by keeping your eyes open. In terms of shopping there could be some bargains about and you are also likely to meet one or two people who could be of use to you. An atmospheric time is likely, and especially so in your dealings with others.

6 THURSDAY
Moon Age Day 6 • Moon Sign Gemini

am ....

pm ....

A loved one can benefit you in a romantic way and there is the chance that the attention you receive from them is going to be of supreme importance in the days to come. The attitudes of friends are somewhat more difficult to judge and to deal with, though you get your head round their needs and wants of you soon enough.

7 FRIDAY

Moon Age Day 7 • Moon Sign Cancer

am ....

pm ....

You show a tendency to look at life through rose-tinted glasses now and will want to do all you can to make the world a much better place than it appears to be in a day to day sense. All that is really wrong is that you are out of sorts with yourself. What you really need is time out to take a little rest.

8 SATURDAY

Moon Age Day 8 • Moon Sign Cancer

am ....

pm ....

A stimulating and interesting meeting of minds is something that you look for at this juncture and you can find exactly the right sort of people to offer you the stimulus that you require to deal with the needs and wants of the day. Keep a low profile in practical matters, which do not suit you just at present.

9 SUNDAY

Moon Age Day 9 • Moon Sign Cancer

am ....

pm ....

This would be the best time of all for getting new projects underway and for making more space for yourself and the sort of life that you choose to live. Once you have dealt with certain social situations which you know to be of great importance, you can devote most of your time to plans for the future as a whole.

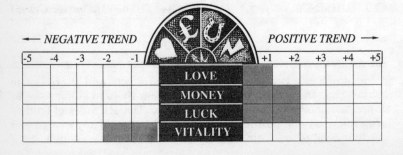

← NEGATIVE TREND							POSITIVE TREND →			
-5	-4	-3	-2	-1		+1	+2	+3	+4	+5
					LOVE					
					MONEY					
					LUCK					
					VITALITY					

10 MONDAY
Moon Age Day 10 • Moon Sign Leo

am ....

pm ....

The new week comes along at a time when you have achieved the sort of physical peak that comes along all too rarely. If you find that not everyone is quite as helpful as they might be, you do at least have the energy to do something about the situation. A reasonable attitude is an important part of your nature now.

11 TUESDAY
Moon Age Day 11 • Moon Sign Leo

am ....

pm ....

You can take great advantage of a situation that comes your way now and should also find that friends and colleagues alike are in the right mood to help you out. Not everyone you come across is equally worthy of your trust however and so strangers should be dealt with more carefully than those you know very well.

12 WEDNESDAY
Moon Age Day 12 • Moon Sign Virgo

am ....

pm ....

You can take great advantage of a personal trust that is being placed in you, since it may also provide information that will be useful for the future. Contradictions do crop up in you life at this time, though they should do little to have any bearing on your attitude in a practical sense.

13 THURSDAY
Moon Age Day 13 • Moon Sign Virgo

am ....

pm ....

Pleasure trips are more or less certain to suit you now, and to carry with them offers that you would find very difficult to refuse. Constant attention to detail could easily get on your nerves at present, which is part of the reason why you decide to ring the changes more or less whenever you are able to do so.

14 FRIDAY
Moon Age Day 14 • Moon Sign Libra

am ....

pm ....

Meetings or appointments regarding certain issues that you know to be of supreme importance should be dealt with as soon as you have the chance to get them out of the way. You need time later in the day to be yourself and to do those things that you know to be of significance in a personal, rather than a professional sense.

15 SATURDAY
Moon Age Day 15 • Moon Sign Libra

am ....

pm ....

The good feelings that you have today could well rub off on those who are the closest to you in a personal or a romantic sense. Give and take are both very important of course, but you will require more determination if you want to push through changes that have had to wait for a while. Someone has an attitude problem.

16 SUNDAY
Moon Age Day 16 • Moon Sign Scorpio

am ....

pm ....

Avoid a tendency to be more lazy than you know to be good for you. There are advantages to taking a rest today it's true, though that does not mean that you should allow yourself to put things off that you know to be of real importance in a daily sense. It might be best to put in your best effort early on.

← NEGATIVE TREND						POSITIVE TREND →				
-5	-4	-3	-2	-1		+1	+2	+3	+4	+5
					LOVE					
					MONEY					
					LUCK					
					VITALITY					

17 MONDAY
Moon Age Day 17 • Moon Sign Scorpio

am ....

pm ....

New information comes to light regarding the behaviour or attitudes of loved ones, and this could radically alter your perception of them in the days that lie ahead. A good heart to heart talk could be all you need in order to come to terms with them and may also explain further facts you have been in the dark about.

18 TUESDAY
Moon Age Day 18 • Moon Sign Sagittarius

am ....

pm ....

You may need to find a suitable alternative outlet for some of your energy, the level of which is higher than has probably been the case for a number of days. You won't take very kindly to routines of any sort and will want to do what you can to stimulate a new interest in facts that lie beyond the common-place.

19 WEDNESDAY
Moon Age Day 19 • Moon Sign Sagittarius

am ....

pm ....

Hopeful news of some kind arrives from a distance, and you are also feeling especially chatty when it comes to dealing with those who are closer to home. A sudden reversal of fortunes, albeit in a small way, could well find you slightly better off financially than you expected to be and friends turn out to be helpful.

20 THURSDAY
Moon Age Day 20 • Moon Sign Capricorn

am ....

pm ....

A new and interesting period comes along with regard to professional developments, and it is one that is assisted by the present position of the sun in your solar tenth house. Try to avoid being overbearing in the way that you deal with others, even though you know that what you are thinking and doing does make sense.

21 FRIDAY
Moon Age Day 21 • Moon Sign Capricorn

am ....

pm ....

There may be serious doubts about today and some of them catch up with you in a way that you do not expect. Work things out in a rational way and do what you can to deal with a slight personal problem that has been hanging about for a while. The more rational you are able to be, the better you deal with situations.

22 SATURDAY
Moon Age Day 22 • Moon Sign Capricorn

am ....

pm ....

Social matters prove to be pleasurable and turn the tide in your favour as far as the general feel of life is concerned. You don't have the general level of energy that you might wish and this means that you may have to pace yourself a little. Some rest and relaxation would turn out to be advantageous.

23 SUNDAY
Moon Age Day 23 • Moon Sign Aquarius

am ....

pm ....

A colleague, or perhaps even your partner, is able to see things from a sensible and concerned view-point today and so the advice they have to offer could prove to be very useful to you. Confidence is not quite what it should be for you, and this is yet another reason why some small reliance on others would help.

← *NEGATIVE TREND*								*POSITIVE TREND* →		
-5	-4	-3	-2	-1		+1	+2	+3	+4	+5
					LOVE					
					MONEY					
					LUCK					
					VITALITY					

24 MONDAY
Moon Age Day 24 • Moon Sign Aquarius

am ....

pm ....

You need to get close to loved ones today, and to be able to share what they are as people. This means having to leave more practical matters alone for a while, no matter how much you want to get on with things. A slightly mysterious situation needs looking at in some detail and lady luck is on your side.

25 TUESDAY
Moon Age Day 25 • Moon Sign Pisces

am ....

pm ....

Tricky decisions have to be made, and since you are now in the right frame of mind to deal with them, you would be well advised, not only to get your thinking cap on, but also to have a chat with people who could turn out to be real experts in their own field. Keep yourself happy and contented outside of work.

26 WEDNESDAY
Moon Age Day 26 • Moon Sign Pisces

am ....

pm ....

Argumentative tendencies are on display now and this could cause you some problems when it comes to dealing with people who you have contact with in a daily sense. The best course of action, in almost any case of confrontation, is to bite your lip and say as little as you can. Tomorrow is better for talking things through.

27 THURSDAY
Moon Age Day 27 • Moon Sign Aries

am ....

pm ....

Though there is much to deal with today in terms of details, most of the facts and figures that you are dealing with are easy to cope with and bring their own sort of rewards in the longer-term. Perhaps this would be a good time to let others lend a hand.

28 FRIDAY

Moon Age Day 28 • Moon Sign Aries

am ....

pm ....

There may be new social encounters about, some of which prove to be especially satisfying at this time. You are able and willing to mix with people from all sorts of backgrounds and circumstances and will find yourself in the mainstream of some interesting events. You should be at your boldest right now.

29 SATURDAY

Moon Age Day 0 • Moon Sign Taurus

am ....

pm ....

Keep to tried and tested paths when it comes to dealing with your life as a whole. This really is not a good day to be sticking your neck out or for doing anything that you know is not sensible. The more you are able to keep yourself to yourself, the less is the possibility of complications arising.

30 SUNDAY

Moon Age Day 1 • Moon Sign Taurus

am ....

pm ....

Career and professional matters are on your mind, even though, this being a Sunday, there may be very little that you can do about them. You stand on the outside of certain family situations and will want to keep things that way for a day or two at least. With friends you will be trying to have a greater influence.

← NEGATIVE TREND   POSITIVE TREND →

-5	-4	-3	-2	-1		+1	+2	+3	+4	+5
					LOVE					
					MONEY					
					LUCK					
					VITALITY					

1995

YOUR MONTH AT A GLANCE

The twelve numbered boxes represent the important areas in your life. The key to the numbers you will find beneath the panel. A Sun above the number indicates that opportunities are around. A Cloud below the number, that you should be a bit defensive. Nothing above or below and life will be pretty ordinary.

			☀	☀					☀		
1	2	3	4	5	6	7	8	9	10	11	12
									☁		

KEY

1 Strength of Personality
2 Personal Finance
3 Useful Information Gathering
4 Domestic Affairs
5 Pleasure & Romance
6 Effective Work & Health

7 One to One Relationships
8 Questioning, Thinking & Deciding
9 External Influences / Education
10 Career Aspirations
11 Teamwork Activities
12 Unconscious Impulses

MAY HIGHS AND LOWS

Here, I show how the rhythm of the Moon will affect you this month. Like the tide, your energies and abilities will rise and fall with its pattern. When it is above the date line, go-for-it. When it is below the line you should be resting.

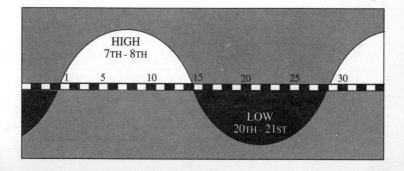

1 MONDAY

Moon Age Day 2 • Moon Sign Taurus

am ....

pm ....

Cooperative or group ventures of any sort are likely to be going your way as the new week gets started. Don't be afraid to take matters into your own hands if you know this to be the best course of action and do whatever is necessary to get new projects off to a flying start. Personal matters should be more settled.

2 TUESDAY

Moon Age Day 3 • Moon Sign Gemini

am ....

pm ....

Verbal and intellectual exchanges take place, some of them having a bearing on you and your life as a whole. This is an excellent time for starting any new sort of project and doing things that you know to be of singular importance to yourself. Thinking about others might mean having to be a little selfish in the first instance.

3 WEDNESDAY

Moon Age Day 4 • Moon Sign Gemini

am ....

pm ....

Your attempts to get ahead in life meet with a few obstacles and some extra effort is required if you want to get the most out of life. The middle of the week seems like something of an island in a storm-tossed sea and this is a good place to be to think things through in a logical and uncluttered way.

4 THURSDAY

Moon Age Day 5 • Moon Sign Gemini

am ....

pm ....

The emphasis now is on personal and even private matters, as you put the needs of others onto the shelf for just a few short hours. Catching up with yourself is important sometimes and you should not feel too bad about closing down the shutters to the world outside for just a short while. Your partner could be mystified however.

5 FRIDAY
Moon Age Day 6 • Moon Sign Cancer

am ....

pm ....

Positive and professional results come through today, as you find yourself back into the swing of life and able to give everything you have to the more practical aspects of your life. At home you are happy, and probably planning for the weekend. A greater than average desire from others to demand your attention could irritate.

6 SATURDAY
Moon Age Day 7 • Moon Sign Cancer

am ....

pm ....

You can enjoy the best of both worlds on this Saturday, since your personal and your social life are both working out extremely well. Those closest to you are easy to deal with and you find that there are advantages to be gained from even the most casual chat. Domestic routines may be forgotten for just a short while.

7 SUNDAY
Moon Age Day 8 • Moon Sign Leo

am ....

pm ....

Put your best foot forward and you will discover that there is progress to be made in directions that you never even considered before. There is plenty of incentive to get ahead now and this is achieved by taking the necessary time out to look ahead and to plan the aspects of life that fall within your own influence.

← *NEGATIVE TREND*   *POSITIVE TREND* →

-5	-4	-3	-2	-1		+1	+2	+3	+4	+5
					LOVE					
					MONEY					
					LUCK					
					VITALITY					

8 MONDAY   *Moon Age Day 9 • Moon Sign Leo*

am ....

pm ....

Your powers of concentration are high and you should find yourself able to cope with the sort of pressures that have troubled even you at some stage in the past. Concentration comes easily and lady luck should be on your side if you decide to embark on any new sort of project in the days to come.

9 TUESDAY   *Moon Age Day 10 • Moon Sign Virgo*

am ....

pm ....

Joint finances could pose certain difficulties and you will be doing all that you can to make certain that they are sorted out as quickly and efficiently as possible. This means being willing to talk, something that you may be reticent to do, especially if your partner or other family members refuse to cooperate.

10 WEDNESDAY   *Moon Age Day 11 • Moon Sign Virgo*

am ....

pm ....

The fighter within your nature is on display today, though there is no real reason for understanding just why this should be the case. The result is that you are sometimes taking actions that are not too sensible and might be inclined to shout the odds before it is necessary to do so. Arguments prove nothing now.

11 THURSDAY   *Moon Age Day 12 • Moon Sign Virgo*

am ....

pm ....

A matter that you have been speculating on comes good, leaving you feeling that life is working out more or less as you have planned. Actions speak louder than words when it comes to dealing with loved ones, some of whom are now more willing to see sense in what you area saying and in the projects you have in hand.

12 FRIDAY
Moon Age Day 13 • Moon Sign Libra

am ....

pm ....

Career and ambitions are uppermost in your mind as the working week draws to a close and it is these areas of life that occupy your mind more than any other today. Some of your reactions may not be quite as considered as you would wish them to be and on a few occasions it would be worth counting to ten before you speak out.

13 SATURDAY
Moon Age Day 14 • Moon Sign Libra

am ....

pm ....

Practical agreements become possible as you adopt a more reasoned and sensible role now. There are advantages to be gained from doing those things that you know to be right for yourself, since in the main they turn out to be appropriate to the people you love too.

14 SUNDAY
Moon Age Day 15 • Moon Sign Scorpio

am ....

pm ....

Unexpected domestic demands come along and might take some of the shine off what could be an otherwise fairly easy-going sort of Sunday. Reasoning is good and there are people about who would be more than willing to listen to what you have to say. If there is any problem, it stems from not knowing yourself all that well.

← *NEGATIVE TREND*   *POSITIVE TREND* →

-5	-4	-3	-2	-1			+1	+2	+3	+4	+5
					LOVE						
					MONEY						
					LUCK						
					VITALITY						

15 MONDAY

Moon Age Day 16 • Moon Sign Scorpio

am ....

pm ....

It seems likely that you positively expect people to lead you up the garden path right now, especially at work. Life being what it is, it probably will not let you down and the very best attitude that you could adopt is to look for the best in others, instead of the worst. Relatives are particularly caring now.

16 TUESDAY

Moon Age Day 17 • Moon Sign Sagittarius

am ....

pm ....

The social atmosphere at work is especially good, and that allows you a platform from which you can spring into the future. Harmony is the order of the day and there are events going on in a social sense that you will not want to miss at any cost. You are able to talk others round to a sensible point of view quite easily.

17 WEDNESDAY

Moon Age Day 18 • Moon Sign Sagittarius

am ....

pm ....

Personal relationships appear to be going especially well now, the more so because you are so willing to see an alternative and sensible point of view. The more caring aspects of your sign are really showing out and these allow you to display your genuine warmth in almost everything that you do.

18 THURSDAY

Moon Age Day 19 • Moon Sign Capricorn

am ....

pm ....

The atmosphere regarding practical matters leaves you with a business as usual approach to the day, which in most other respects turns out to be quite uneventful. Be as adventurous as you know how to be and try to swing the balance away from routines, which have little to offer you at the present time.

19 FRIDAY
Moon Age Day 20 • Moon Sign Capricorn

am ....

pm ....

Your emotional sensitivity is stimulated to the full and you turn with love towards those people who have your best interests as much at heart as you do theirs. This is a day for sharing, both in terms of what you have and what you know. An active and enterprising phase is on the way and becomes obvious by evening.

20 SATURDAY
Moon Age Day 21 • Moon Sign Aquarius

am ....

pm ....

The business of the day is subject to certain hold-ups about which you can do almost nothing. It may be best to shelve important discussions of one sort or another until a later date, in favour of simply enjoying today for what it offers in a more casual sense. Give and take are important when dealing with younger people.

21 SUNDAY
Moon Age Day 22 • Moon Sign Aquarius

am ....

pm ....

A more determined attitude is now called for, even though this might be a little difficult to find at first. Cooperation in a family sense is also the name of the game, but there are people about who seem less than willing to join in, at least for a short while. Rules and regulations are inclined to get on your nerves.

← NEGATIVE TREND						POSITIVE TREND →				
-5	-4	-3	-2	-1		+1	+2	+3	+4	+5
					LOVE					
					MONEY					
					LUCK					
					VITALITY					

22 MONDAY

Moon Age Day 23 • Moon Sign Pisces

am ....

pm ....

The sun moves into your solar eleventh house and the general pattern is one of personal fulfilment during the the next month or so. It's plain that you will not want to push over any buses at present, though it is also likely that you will find yourself in a position that allows you to consolidate past gains.

23 TUESDAY

Moon Age Day 24 • Moon Sign Pisces

am ....

pm ....

A physical peak can be expected, so it is a case of getting anything that you can done whilst the going is good. A refusal to listen to what other people are saying of little use to you at present and you would be better advised to sit still for a few moments and take in the implications of an alternative view-point.

24 WEDNESDAY

Moon Age Day 25 • Moon Sign Aries

am ....

pm ....

There may be time to vary your everyday routines in order to find more time for yourself, something that may not have been too possible in the recent past. Confidence to do whatever you want is around, even if you have to search hard in order to find it. A greater sense of purpose is now possible, though effort is required.

25 THURSDAY

Moon Age Day 26 • Moon Sign Aries

am ....

pm ....

There is no doubt at all that your popularity is at a peak, and that makes this an excellent time for getting your own way. Such is your nature however that you will not try to do so at the expense of others, many of whom are also in a position to help you out. Brave responses to apparent troubles are called for.

26 FRIDAY
Moon Age Day 27 • Moon Sign Aries

am ....

pm ....

Typical Leonine extravagance is to be expected now, and it is
something that you would be well advised to fight against whenever
you can. The needs of those around you do tend to predominate for a
short while and you can be certain that you will not let anyone down
if they really show a need of your help.

27 SATURDAY
Moon Age Day 28 • Moon Sign Taurus

am ....

pm ....

Friendship issues are significant and take priority over almost
anything right at the moment. You may have jobs to do around the
house, though you would be well advised to seek out the help and
support of others before you undertake them. Take a long hard look
at the amount of money you are spending at present.

28 SUNDAY
Moon Age Day 29 • Moon Sign Taurus

am ....

pm ....

Important projects have to wait for a while, since you are not really
in the mood to sort them out right now. Sunday offers you the
chance to look at things more realistically and to come to terms with
changes that you know are on the horizon. Comfort and general
security are two factors that also play a part in your thinking.

← NEGATIVE TREND						POSITIVE TREND →				
-5	-4	-3	-2	-1		+1	+2	+3	+4	+5
					LOVE					
					MONEY					
					LUCK					
					VITALITY					

115

29 MONDAY   *Moon Age Day 0 • Moon Sign Gemini*

am ....

pm ....

A gathering of friends offers you some light-hearted moments at some stage early in this week, and probably today. The news that they have to impart starts you thinking in new directions and possibly ones that are of genuine assistance to you for some days or weeks to come. Go for gold in any sort of sporting endeavour.

30 TUESDAY   *Moon Age Day 1 • Moon Sign Gemini*

am ....

pm ....

Social occasions could fail to live up to your expectations of them, and this is one reason why you will want to do whatever you can to enliven the possibilities on an otherwise uninspiring day. Not everyone is all that willing to join in with your efforts, but with a little persuasion it is wonderful how they may react.

31 WEDNESDAY   *Moon Age Day 2 • Moon Sign Gemini*

am ....

pm ....

A slightly irritable and probably pessimistic attitude could easily take you over before the day is out, something that you will want to avoid at all cost. Of course it is hard to go against tendencies that are not really of your own making and these impulses, though only an interlude, have to be accepted.

1 THURSDAY   *Moon Age Day 3 • Moon Sign Cancer*

am ....

pm ....

Expect a day of fairly high spirits, as a contrast to yesterday. All aspects of leisure have a part to play in the way that you mind is working and help to lift your spirits on this May Thursday. Not everyone you encounter is equally happy however and you may find that much of the day is spent encouraging others.

2 FRIDAY

Moon Age Day 4 • Moon Sign Cancer

am ....

pm ....

A general lack of confidence finds you once again inclined not to expect the best from yourself, or in the mood to go out and get it. Realising what you are capable of, you are still inclined to err on the side of caution when it comes to self-belief. What you need is a greater degree of Leo determination.

3 SATURDAY

Moon Age Day 5 • Moon Sign Leo

am ....

pm ....

There is a strong element of luck about in your life at present, something that allows you to look forward in a way that has not been possible for quite a few days now. Be as adventurous as you know how to be and allow yourself the chance to take pot-luck over issues that have been on your mind for a while.

4 SUNDAY

Moon Age Day 6 • Moon Sign Leo

am ....

pm ....

New ideas are up your sleeve and though it is not at all easy to put them into practice for today at least, there is nothing to prevent you from getting out a pen and paper and looking at them in a positive light. Reactions are quick and you will not stand for people trying to pull the wool over your eyes at any stage.

← *NEGATIVE TREND*   *POSITIVE TREND* →

-5	-4	-3	-2	-1			+1	+2	+3	+4	+5
					LOVE						
					MONEY						
					LUCK						
					VITALITY						

1995

YOUR MONTH AT A GLANCE

The twelve numbered boxes represent the important areas in your life. The key to the numbers you will find beneath the panel. A Sun above the number indicates that opportunities are around. A Cloud below the number, that you should be a bit defensive. Nothing above or below and life will be pretty ordinary.

☀						☀		☀		
1	2	3	4	5	6	7	8	9	10	11	12
		☁						☁			

KEY

1 Strength of Personality
2 Personal Finance
3 Useful Information Gathering
4 Domestic Affairs
5 Pleasure & Romance
6 Effective Work & Health
7 One to One Relationships
8 Questioning, Thinking & Deciding
9 External Influences / Education
10 Career Aspirations
11 Teamwork Activities
12 Unconscious Impulses

JUNE HIGHS AND LOWS

Here, I show how the rhythm of the Moon will affect you this month. Like the tide, your energies and abilities will rise and fall with its pattern. When it is above the date line, go-for-it. When it is below the line you should be resting.

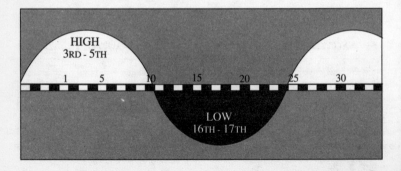

HIGH
3RD - 5TH

1   5   10   15   20   25   30

LOW
16TH - 17TH

5 MONDAY   *Moon Age Day 7 • Moon Sign Leo*

am ....

pm ....

This is a day when you really need to feel that you are fully in control of all situations, and especially those that have a bearing on your life in a financial sense. When it comes to confiding in others, better the devil you know than the one you don't, though do be careful who you talk to all the same.

6 TUESDAY   *Moon Age Day 8 • Moon Sign Virgo*

am ....

pm ....

Don't become any more concerned with the lives of other people, and especially strangers, than you really have to. It may feel to you as if you are resting on your laurels more than would normally be the case, but everyone has to have rest from time to time and you are really no exception.

7 WEDNESDAY   *Moon Age Day 9 • Moon Sign Virgo*

am ....

pm ....

There is always more than one way to make progress, and especially so for you in a professional sense today. Take what others have to say on board and use the experiences of their lives as a yardstick when it comes to thinking about your own. Conventions are not very rewarding now, so do be different.

8 THURSDAY   *Moon Age Day 10 • Moon Sign Libra*

am ....

pm ....

A friend or a social contact could well come to you with a hard luck story and it will be all that you can do not to find yourself crying in a corner with them. Fortunately the more practical aspect of your nature takes over and you should find yourself in a position to help and rectify matters.

9 FRIDAY

Moon Age Day 11 • Moon Sign Libra

am ....

pm ....

Don't allow loved ones or family members to get the upper hand, and especially not when you know that what they are saying or doing goes against the grain with you personally. Professional developments deserve a light touch, and you could find that there are options available to you that would not have thought possible.

10 SATURDAY

Moon Age Day 12 • Moon Sign Scorpio

am ....

pm ....

A matter close to your own heart is worth talking about today, no matter who it is that you find yourself associated with. Even the most unlikely individuals can come good at present and should be in a position to offer advice that is both sensible and considered. Give and take are important in personal relationships.

11 SUNDAY

Moon Age Day 13 • Moon Sign Scorpio

am ....

pm ....

A new though minor boost to social matters starts you looking at life in a very different way, probably because you are mixing with the sort of people who have similar ideas to your own. Carving out a niche for yourself in life appeals to you just at present and there are options about now to do just that.

← NEGATIVE TREND							POSITIVE TREND →			
-5	-4	-3	-2	-1			+1	+2	+3	+4	+5
					LOVE					
					MONEY					
					LUCK					
					VITALITY					

12 MONDAY
Moon Age Day 14 • Moon Sign Sagittarius

am ....

pm ....

Today marks one of the most carefree modes that Leo is liable to enjoy at any stage this month. Get out and about as much as you can, enjoying what life has to offer in the state of abandon that is typical of your sign. Making the most of your free time means being able to get masses done, and in an enjoyable way too!

13 TUESDAY
Moon Age Day 15 • Moon Sign Sagittarius

am ....

pm ....

You seem determined to have a slice of the action at present, whatever that represents to you personally. A sudden change in circumstances finds you on top form and able to do all sorts of things that you may have avoided previously. This is a good day to be a Leo, and a happy time is available at home.

14 WEDNESDAY
Moon Age Day 16 • Moon Sign Capricorn

am ....

pm ....

Work and all practical matters are helped along by a more adventurous attitude on the part of those who you mix with the most. Arrange things so that you have more time to spend with loved ones and friends too. If it proves to be possible to mix personal and social life, then so much the better at this stage.

15 THURSDAY
Moon Age Day 17 • Moon Sign Capricorn

am ....

pm ....

You will find that there is some confusion surrounding you at present and there may well be little that you can do to alter the situation. The secret may well be to go with the flow and to accept what life has on offer, even if you do not really care for it all that much. A more free and easy attitude is required.

16 FRIDAY

Moon Age Day 18 • Moon Sign Aquarius

am ....

pm ....

Beware of thinking that the grass is greener elsewhere, because in reality it almost certainly is not. Keeping up appearances is a fact of life right now and the lion tends to preen itself in public more than would usually be the case. Reacting to arguments that originate elsewhere really doesn't get you very far.

17 SATURDAY

Moon Age Day 19 • Moon Sign Aquarius

am ....

pm ....

A partner or a colleague may have to be drafted in to help you out with something that you are not certain about yourself. An active and happy period is around for the taking and you should find that the weekend turns out to be everything that you expected. Silence is not for you at present, so keep talking.

18 SUNDAY

Moon Age Day 20 • Moon Sign Pisces

am ....

pm ....

A friend or a relative makes a gesture that you find to be especially touching and for which you could well decide to pay them back. Comfort is on your mind and you may decide that this is a stay at home sort of day. Other family members are likely to have different ideas however, especially at first.

← *NEGATIVE TREND*   *POSITIVE TREND* →

-5	-4	-3	-2	-1		+1	+2	+3	+4	+5
					LOVE					
					MONEY					
					LUCK					
					VITALITY					

19 MONDAY   *Moon Age Day 21 • Moon Sign Pisces*

am ....

pm ....

A day to strike out on your own and certainly not a good time for allowing others to decide how you should live your life. If they do you could find yourself becoming a little angry and since this really would not help any situation, it would be sensible to count to ten before you allow yourself to react harshly.

20 TUESDAY   *Moon Age Day 22 • Moon Sign Pisces*

am ....

pm ....

An easy-going and carefree sort of day appears to be on the cards, and there is plenty to keep you occupied in a multitude of ways. The confidence to do whatever you want is certainly not lacking at present and you have all the incentive in the world to push the frontiers of your life onward and upward in the days ahead.

21 WEDNESDAY   *Moon Age Day 23 • Moon Sign Aries*

am ....

pm ....

A generally introspective phase takes you by surprise and may stop you in your tracks right now. There may be nothing to do but to accept the situation and to deal with it as best you can. It's true that you will not get through everything that you want but you can be fairly certain that at least social aspects look promising.

22 THURSDAY   *Moon Age Day 24 • Moon Sign Aries*

am ....

pm ....

The emphasis now is on pleasure for its own sake and you are in a position to put your best foot forward. Don't go over the top when it comes to dealing with others because you could be just a little too adventurous and inclined to promise more than you can actually offer.

23 FRIDAY

Moon Age Day 25 • Moon Sign Taurus

am ....

pm ....

Today marks a time of heavy responsibilities and one on which you will be doing all that you can to remedy the situation, probably by a combination of hard work and steady application to the job in hand. You may feel the need to compartment your life more than is really necessary, since your powers of concentration are good.

24 SATURDAY

Moon Age Day 26 • Moon Sign Taurus

am ....

pm ....

You attract those people who have the most to say for themselves, but who can be of very definite use to you for now. A continued search for your own identity in life is now going to lead you down paths that you never even knew existed previously. Ideas are coming in thick and fast.

25 SUNDAY

Moon Age Day 27 • Moon Sign Taurus

am ....

pm ....

A financial matter has to dealt with as soon as you are able to get your head round to sorting it out. Try not to spend more than you have to today and be careful when it comes to taking any sort of risk that has short or long-term financial implications. You are very active socially, once responsibilities are out of the way.

← NEGATIVE TREND						POSITIVE TREND →				
-5	-4	-3	-2	-1		+1	+2	+3	+4	+5
					LOVE					
					MONEY					
					LUCK					
					VITALITY					

26 MONDAY
Moon Age Day 28 • Moon Sign Gemini

am ....

pm ....

Feelings of duty and a sense of responsibility generally press in heavily on you today and could prevent you from making as much out of life as you would really wish. Don't indulge yourself too much at the moment and do be prepared to leave certain tasks alone until you know that there is more stamina available.

27 TUESDAY
Moon Age Day 29 • Moon Sign Gemini

am ....

pm ....

Your public image is something that you will want to work on, though in reality you are enjoying a happy time when it comes to the attention that comes from others. Realistically you should be working hard at present, making the most of every new opportunity that comes your way. In reality, you may feel lazy.

28 WEDNESDAY
Moon Age Day 0 • Moon Sign Cancer

am ....

pm ....

Beware of trying to do more than you know to be sensible, since all that will happen as a result is that you will become more stressed than you should. Slow and steady wins the race, even for a Lion, and you should not expect to be in a position to take the world by storm, for the moment at least.

29 THURSDAY
Moon Age Day 1 • Moon Sign Cancer

am ....

pm ....

It would be far too easy to overestimate your own potential, so much so that you could run yourself into difficulties that take some getting out of. A far more positive attitude begins to develop as the day grows older and you can be certain that you have enough energy to cope with any one of a number of eventualities.

30 FRIDAY
Moon Age Day 2 • Moon Sign Cancer

am ....

pm ....

There is now a greater sense of optimism about, and much more of an ability to smile, even in the face of adversity. Any problems that remain tend to be sorted out quite early in the day, leaving you feeling somehow that the decks are cleared for action and that you are in just the right mood to take the world by storm.

1 SATURDAY
Moon Age Day 3 • Moon Sign Leo

am ....

pm ....

This is the best time of all to put enterprising ideas into action, and for taking on a world that looks far more promising than it probably has for a couple of weeks or more. With general good luck on the increase, you need to feel that everything you are doing serves a valuable purpose and is tackled with a sensible approach.

2 SUNDAY
Moon Age Day 4 • Moon Sign Leo

am ....

pm ....

Focus upon important practical matters and put your mind to the test concerning projects that cannot be commenced now, but which have their day before very long. The number of rewards that come your way in the longer-term justify the way that you are willing to think long and hard now about your life as a whole.

← *NEGATIVE TREND*							*POSITIVE TREND* →			
-5	-4	-3	-2	-1			+1	+2	+3	+4	+5
					LOVE						
					MONEY						
					LUCK						
					VITALITY						

1995

YOUR MONTH AT A GLANCE

The twelve numbered boxes represent the important areas in your life. The key to the numbers you will find beneath the panel. A Sun above the number indicates that opportunities are around. A Cloud below the number, that you should be a bit defensive. Nothing above or below and life will be pretty ordinary.

| 1 | 2 | 3 | 4 | 5 | 6 | 7 | 8 | 9 | 10 | 11 | 12 |

KEY

1 Strength of Personality	7 One to One Relationships
2 Personal Finance	8 Questioning, Thinking & Deciding
3 Useful Information Gathering	9 External Influences / Education
4 Domestic Affairs	10 Career Aspirations
5 Pleasure & Romance	11 Teamwork Activities
6 Effective Work & Health	12 Unconscious Impulses

JULY HIGHS AND LOWS

Here, I show how the rhythm of the Moon will affect you this month. Like the tide, your energies and abilities will rise and fall with its pattern. When it is above the date line, go-for-it. When it is below the line you should be resting.

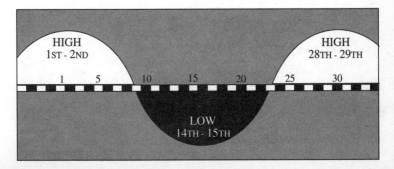

3 MONDAY

Moon Age Day 5 • Moon Sign Virgo

am ....

pm ....

An active time to the week, and one that proves to be far more enterprising than you would expect, is what you find today. A continuation of the generally favourable trends that ended last week can be expected, even if today is not exactly ideal for trying to bite of more than you can realistically chew.

4 TUESDAY

Moon Age Day 6 • Moon Sign Virgo

am ....

pm ....

You need to feel free to explore relationships in any way that takes your fancy now and will be allowed by others to do so. A more free and easy attitude to life as a whole finds you anxious to mix with almost anyone who will talk to you, which is just about everyone you meet. Confidence is rising by the day.

5 WEDNESDAY

Moon Age Day 7 • Moon Sign Libra

am ....

pm ....

It is possible that you will be just a little too sensitive about the remarks that are made by others, not a state of affairs that would do you much good at this point in time. If you have any paperwork to do, this would be the most opportune time to be getting on with it, and is also an ideal time to write letters.

6 THURSDAY

Moon Age Day 8 • Moon Sign Libra

am ....

pm ....

This may be a more relaxing time than you realistically expect, and that means time to stop and think about things more than has been possible for a while. Everyone knows how lions love to rest in the sun and the zodiac lion is no exception. Try to be on hand to sort out the odd difficulty occuring within the family.

7 FRIDAY

Moon Age Day 9 • Moon Sign Scorpio

am ....

pm ....

Though one-to-one relationships appear to be going much easier than you might have lead yourself to believe during the last few days, there are advantages to looking further from home in terms of the favourable impression you can make on others. Your sympathy for the world at large is much in evidence now.

8 SATURDAY

Moon Age Day 10 • Moon Sign Scorpio

am ....

pm ....

You serve your own best interests today when dealing with the needs and wants of home and family and would not be likely to be wandering further from your own door than proves to be necessary. A continued search for new and interesting aspects within your own nature typifies the approach you take to life at present.

9 SUNDAY

Moon Age Day 11 • Moon Sign Sagittarius

am ....

pm ....

Your personality is genuinely charming at the moment and you have little difficulty winning people round to your point of view. Attending to your own needs and wants is something that comes second right now to thinking about those of the people you care for the most. Their gratitude is a great cause of joy.

← *NEGATIVE TREND*   *POSITIVE TREND* →

-5	-4	-3	-2	-1			+1	+2	+3	+4	+5
					LOVE						
					MONEY						
					LUCK						
					VITALITY						

10 MONDAY *Moon Age Day 12 • Moon Sign Sagittarius*

am ....

pm ....

The kind of positive value judgements that you capable of today show just how much you are able to assess the true potential of the people with whom you live and work. Attempting the impossible might not be such a good idea, though the difficult you can deal with in no time at all. Be prudent with money.

11 TUESDAY *Moon Age Day 13 • Moon Sign Sagittarius*

am ....

pm ....

You could feel that someone is trying to stand in your way and this is not a state of affairs that you are willing to deal with just at the moment. All the same, a little tact might go a long way and you would not do yourself any good at all by refusing to give at least a little ground when you know it is necessary.

12 WEDNESDAY *Moon Age Day 14 • Moon Sign Capricorn*

am ....

pm ....

You may require a more enlightened approach to life than the one you are able to adopt right now. Confusion is likely to take you over at some stage during the day and you find that not everything goes according to plan. All of this is apt to sap your confidence just a little and may prevent much progress.

13 THURSDAY *Moon Age Day 15 • Moon Sign Capricorn*

am ....

pm ....

Your partner, or perhaps a close personal friend, requires more in the way of encouragement at this time. It may be a good idea to let them handle situations that you know you could sort out quite easily for yourself, if only because it allows them a greater degree of confidence in their own abilities.

14 FRIDAY

Moon Age Day 16 • Moon Sign Aquarius

am ....

pm ....

Minor setbacks can be slightly disappointing at this time, though they should be taken with a pinch of salt and not allowed to have the part to play in your life that seems to be the case right now. Even where you do find that there are difficulties to be faced, you tend to be able to sort them out quite easily.

15 SATURDAY

Moon Age Day 17 • Moon Sign Aquarius

am ....

pm ....

The benefits that come from close personal relationships now put you in the right mood to make gains of many different sorts, even far from the implications of the attachments themselves. If you are in the market for a bargain, this could be the best time of the month to go out and get it. Be bold when dealing with strangers.

16 SUNDAY

Moon Age Day 18 • Moon Sign Pisces

am ....

pm ....

For once you prefer to work behind the scenes and will be keeping a much lower profile than might often be the case. Some of your most treasured regimes have to be abandoned for a short while, if only because you know that there are practical considerations that demand your attention. This is not a good time to push your luck.

← *NEGATIVE TREND*						*POSITIVE TREND* →				
-5	-4	-3	-2	-1		+1	+2	+3	+4	+5
					LOVE					
					MONEY					
					LUCK					
					VITALITY					

17 MONDAY

Moon Age Day 19 • Moon Sign Pisces

am ....

pm ....

At the start of a new working week you feel really inspired to go out and get what you want from life. Looking ahead carefully you are able to plan with confidence, knowing that whatever it is that you decide to take on, there will be plenty of energy and know-how to get through it. Love tends to be rewarding.

18 TUESDAY

Moon Age Day 20 • Moon Sign Aries

am ....

pm ....

You may suspect that there are minor dents developing within relationships and if this turns out to be the case, it would be better to deal with them now than to let matters build up too much. You can be especially creative at present and will want to help out with a particular project somewhere close to home.

19 WEDNESDAY

Moon Age Day 21 • Moon Sign Aries

am ....

pm ....

With just a little caution and self-control it is really amazing what you can get through today. Attitudes are changeable, though your desire to succeed is less so. Confronting the alterations that are taking place inside yourself may not be too easy, though you become stronger in your convictions as the week wears on.

20 THURSDAY

Moon Age Day 22 • Moon Sign Taurus

am ....

pm ....

A more forthright approach now works wonders and you are certainly not afraid to tell people what you think. Being out and about as much as possible today, you are able to find all manner of people to talk to and deal with. Confidence is there for the taking and few Leos would turn it away right now.

21 FRIDAY
Moon Age Day 23 • Moon Sign Taurus

am ....

pm ....

The more outspoken tendencies that you show today are in evidence almost from the moment that you get out of bed. In reality it would be better on occasions to hold your tongue because you are likely to say a little more than is really good for you. A break from routines would be good, if you can allow yourself the time.

22 SATURDAY
Moon Age Day 24 • Moon Sign Taurus

am ....

pm ....

Social encounters, parties and gatherings, all have their part to play in this weekend. You are able to show exactly the sort of metal you are made of if you find that there are disputes of any sort to be dealt with. Finding people who are on the same wavelength as others, your communications skills are shining out.

23 SUNDAY
Moon Age Day 25 • Moon Sign Gemini

am ....

pm ....

The sun enters your solar first house and brings with it an important period of personal reward, though mainly it has to be said because you are so willing to go out and look for things yourself. Sooner or later you are going to discover that there are dragons somewhere in your own mind that have to be fought.

	NEGATIVE TREND						POSITIVE TREND			
-5	-4	-3	-2	-1		+1	+2	+3	+4	+5
					LOVE					
					MONEY					
					LUCK					
					VITALITY					

24 MONDAY
Moon Age Day 26 • Moon Sign Gemini

am ....

pm ....

Believing in yourself is the surest key to success in the days that lie ahead and especially so at the start of this new working week. Prepare yourself for one or two encounters that you may not care for the look of just at the moment and think about how you are going react when in the company of people who worry you a little.

25 TUESDAY
Moon Age Day 27 • Moon Sign Cancer

am ....

pm ....

The pace of life and everyday events becomes faster and faster, which should suit your nature down to the ground. Important information comes in from a number of different directions and the only necessary requirement is that you find yourself to be in a position to make the most of it once it arrives.

26 WEDNESDAY
Moon Age Day 28 • Moon Sign Cancer

am ....

pm ....

Though you might wish to slacken the general pace of your life a little, in the main you are anxious to keep up whatever pressure you can muster, especially in a workaday sense. People are willing and anxious to see your point of view and to make the most of all you have to say, so be prepared to speak out.

27 THURSDAY
Moon Age Day 0 • Moon Sign Cancer

am ....

pm ....

Your powerful and dynamic personality attracts all manner of people today and you will soon find that you can talk almost anyone round to a point of view that you know to be both reasonable and valid. Colleagues are unlikely to leave you out in the cold at any time within the next several days.

28 FRIDAY
Moon Age Day 1 • Moon Sign Leo

am ....

pm ....

A physical peak is achieved, and it is one that finds you in just the right frame of mind to get what you want from life, no matter how much this fact might go against the grain where others are concerned. You cannot expect to get on with just anyone at the moment and so you need to be selective in your choice of friends.

29 SATURDAY
Moon Age Day 2 • Moon Sign Leo

am ....

pm ....

A friend or perhaps a colleague is now in a position to do you a great favour, even though you probably have not asked them to do so. When you find that help is at hand, it would be rather foolish to turn it away, especially since the person who is offering it does so willingly and without expectation.

30 SUNDAY
Moon Age Day 3 • Moon Sign Virgo

am ....

pm ....

You are quick to respond to any opportunity that comes your way and would not be at all willing to stand on the sidelines of life any longer than you had to. If you feel any frustrations with life at present it would be unwise to take them out on the people who you are going to have to rely on the most in the days ahead.

←— *NEGATIVE TREND*   *POSITIVE TREND* —→

-5	-4	-3	-2	-1		+1	+2	+3	+4	+5
					LOVE					
					MONEY					
					LUCK					
					VITALITY					

31 MONDAY
Moon Age Day 4 • Moon Sign Virgo

am ....

pm ....

In conversation you can be extremely talkative and quite able to put your point of view in a sensible and lucid manner. Your mind works very quickly and you an jump to the sort of conclusions that even you would find difficult as a rule. Personal remarks that are made to you should not be taken at face value.

1 TUESDAY
Moon Age Day 5 • Moon Sign Virgo

am ....

pm ....

Avoid making decisions regarding matters that you are not familiar with, or you could find that you are quickly out of your depth. For the next day or two it would be sensible to stick to what you know and not to allow yourself to wander too much from the roots of your knowledge. Some extra tact seems to be called for.

2 WEDNESDAY
Moon Age Day 6 • Moon Sign Libra

am ....

pm ....

Busy and energetic, now is the time to be careful that you do not scatter your energies any more than you have to. The more you able to concentrate on one job at once, the better they will eventually be done and out of the way. This turns out to be a rewarding period and one that is set apart from ordinary days.

3 THURSDAY
Moon Age Day 7 • Moon Sign Libra

am ....

pm ....

Where romantic issues are concerned you can really put yourself to the test and should come out feeling that members of the opposite sex find you to be more attractive than you may have previously thought. Expect the best from personal relationships and in the end that is what you are likely to find.

4 FRIDAY
Moon Age Day 8 • Moon Sign Scorpio

am ....

pm ....

You can now be much more accommodating to family members than seems to have been the case for a few days, and with the weekend approaching it is likely that you will be planning to spend more time in their company than has been previously possible. Finish the working week by catching up on jobs left over from the past.

5 SATURDAY
Moon Age Day 9 • Moon Sign Scorpio

am ....

pm ....

Pleasure pursuits and entertainment of all sorts now brings out the best in you and allows you to look with new eyes at the world that surrounds you. All the same, don't allow a taste for the good life prevent you from doing what you know to be right in a practical sense. Rules can be hard to abide by now.

6 SUNDAY
Moon Age Day 10 • Moon Sign Sagittarius

am ....

pm ....

This would be a good time to clear up any misunderstandings that have been around for a while and the arrival of Sunday facilitates even more than this, since it allows you to spend more time with the ones you love the most. A very affectionate Leo is now on display and the day makes a good forerunner to the week to come.

← NEGATIVE TREND						POSITIVE TREND →				
-5	-4	-3	-2	-1		+1	+2	+3	+4	+5
					LOVE					
					MONEY					
					LUCK					
					VITALITY					

1995

YOUR MONTH AT A GLANCE

The twelve numbered boxes represent the important areas in your life. The key to the numbers you will find beneath the panel. A Sun above the number indicates that opportunities are around. A Cloud below the number, that you should be a bit defensive. Nothing above or below and life will be pretty ordinary.

1	2	3	4	5	6	7	8	9	10	11	12

KEY

1 Strength of Personality	7 One to One Relationships
2 Personal Finance	8 Questioning, Thinking & Deciding
3 Useful Information Gathering	9 External Influences / Education
4 Domestic Affairs	10 Career Aspirations
5 Pleasure & Romance	11 Teamwork Activities
6 Effective Work & Health	12 Unconscious Impulses

AUGUST HIGHS AND LOWS

Here, I show how the rhythm of the Moon will affect you this month. Like the tide, your energies and abilities will rise and fall with its pattern. When it is above the date line, go-for-it. When it is below the line you should be resting.

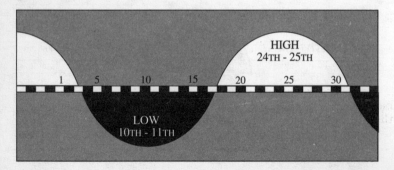

7 MONDAY
Moon Age Day 11 • Moon Sign Sagittarius

am ....

pm ....

A sense of get up and go is hard to miss today and you are certainly in the mood to start the week with a real flourish. Conventions of almost any sort are for the birds and you do everything you can to lift the lives of those you live and work alongside. Confusion from the past is soon left behind.

8 TUESDAY
Moon Age Day 12 • Moon Sign Capricorn

am ....

pm ....

There may be minor disruptions to your routines and you do whatever you can to life the quality of the day, even despite this fact. The common touch is something that you possess in abundance today and so it is possible for you to get on with anyone. Unfortunately, you kindness may not be returned.

9 WEDNESDAY
Moon Age Day 13 • Moon Sign Capricorn

am ....

pm ....

You are especially resourceful today and so should be able to turn most of the situations of your life to you own advantage. You can put new ideas into operation and will want to do all you can to be a shining star, even if the day is a little cloudy in a personal sense. An adventurous streak begins to show.

10 THURSDAY
Moon Age Day 14 • Moon Sign Aquarius

am ....

pm ....

General progress takes a turn for the worse. It isn't that you are behaving any differently from the way that you normally would, simply that others are not. Give and take are really important, though not if it is you who is doing all the giving. An awkward atmosphere at work should soon be left behind.

11 FRIDAY
Moon Age Day 15 • Moon Sign Aquarius

am ....

pm ....

A personal disappointment could come about as a result of putting your faith in the sort of people who are inclined to let you down. Actually judging who these individuals may be is not all that easy at present and you will have to use your intuition to the full in order to work the situation out.

12 SATURDAY
Moon Age Day 16 • Moon Sign Pisces

am ....

pm ....

An excellent period for intimate relationships and for making the most out of any change that is taking place in the structure of your life. Prepare for some changes to your everyday life, and probably ones that involve you in a sequence of events that are not really of your own making or choosing.

13 SUNDAY
Moon Age Day 17 • Moon Sign Pisces

am ....

pm ....

Intellectual debate and the chance to have a good old natter with just about anyone is a stimulus today and offers you a more exciting period from a personal point of view. Don't expect to get too much done in a practical sense and be prepared to take life in your stride, at least for the remainder of today.

← NEGATIVE TREND							POSITIVE TREND →			
-5	-4	-3	-2	-1		+1	+2	+3	+4	+5
					LOVE					
					MONEY					
					LUCK					
					VITALITY					

14 MONDAY

Moon Age Day 18 • Moon Sign Aries

am ....

pm ....

Blind faith is not much use to you now when it comes to making important decisions. You would be far better advised to seek the support of friends, and particularly those who are specialists in a field that may be of particular concern to you at present. A combination of good sense and intuition could come to your aid.

15 TUESDAY

Moon Age Day 19 • Moon Sign Aries

am ....

pm ....

You are now able to achieve a physical peak, and it is one that promises much in terms of the level of energy that it offers and the incentives that become a possibility because of it. The reactions of friends could be somewhat surprising on occasions and you really do have to take them with a pinch of salt.

16 WEDNESDAY

Moon Age Day 20 • Moon Sign Aries

am ....

pm ....

Confidence is certainly not all that you would wish it to be, which is why you would be well advised to slow things down a little and to take a more steady approach to life as a whole. The middle of the week does at least allow you some time for reflection and to look at certain situations again.

17 THURSDAY

Moon Age Day 21 • Moon Sign Taurus

am ....

pm ....

An employer looks upon your efforts in a favourable light at present and so this is an ideal time to put in that extra bit of work which gets you noticed. Don't be surprised if new and interesting offers are on the table, and avoid turning them down out of hand, at least until you have had a look at them.

141

18 FRIDAY
Moon Age Day 22 • Moon Sign Taurus

am ....

pm ....

Your partner, or a loved one, could easily fail to live up to your expectations of them today and that means that you could react in a
less than fortunate way regarding them. Any difficulties that do
arise in relationships are unlikely to last very long and there is no
reason whatsoever for reacting adversely.

19 SATURDAY
Moon Age Day 23 • Moon Sign Gemini

am ....

pm ....

Teamwork and cooperative ventures of almost any sort go more
smoothly than you could possibly believe and that means that this is
an area of your life that should be followed through. A good time for
shopping, or for hunting out bargains in the least expected places.
Someone special may enter your life soon.

20 SUNDAY
Moon Age Day 24 • Moon Sign Gemini

am ....

pm ....

You are impatient when it comes to restrictions of any sort and will
want to do all you can to make certain that things go according to
plan. This may not be all that easy to achieve on a Sunday and some
patience is necessary if you are not to lose your temper with others.
Don't deny yourself the right to be changeable though.

←— *NEGATIVE TREND*   *POSITIVE TREND* —→

-5	-4	-3	-2	-1		+1	+2	+3	+4	+5
					LOVE					
					MONEY					
					LUCK					
					VITALITY					

21 MONDAY
Moon Age Day 25 • Moon Sign Gemini

am ....

pm ....

You may not be looking at things with quite the level of realism that is usually typical of your nature, and this is just one of the reasons why this would not be at all a good time for making decisions of any really serious sort. A short period of solitude could turn out to be especially helpful at some stage.

22 TUESDAY
Moon Age Day 26 • Moon Sign Cancer

am ....

pm ....

Social matters are on your mind now and this is the area of your life that really finds you shining out like a star. Almost everyone you come across is pleased to know you and to offer you the right to make important decisions. The more you mix with others, the better the results of your life should be.

23 WEDNESDAY
Moon Age Day 27 • Moon Sign Cancer

am ....

pm ....

Rewards now come in thick and fast, and not all of them from the sort of direction that you might be expecting. There may be something that you have to say to a family member, even if to do so entails some sort of journey. People are generally very interested to know what makes you tick, but do you know?

24 THURSDAY
Moon Age Day 28 • Moon Sign Leo

am ....

pm ....

An extra element of luck is on your side, not only today but for several more to come. As a result you find this to be the ideal period for being willing to take a chance and for pushing your good luck to the absolute limits. Many of the events of today, even awkward ones, turn out to be a blessing in disguise.

25 FRIDAY
Moon Age Day 29 • Moon Sign Leo

am ....

pm ....

Your partner, or someone else you are especially close to, can bring the sort of news into your life that you have been waiting for for some time. Even casual news has a part to play in your thinking and you should discover that you have more influence in your own life than has appeared to be the case for quite a while.

26 SATURDAY
Moon Age Day 0 • Moon Sign Virgo

am ....

pm ....

The present position of Venus stimulates you into a search for pleasure and relaxation. Confidence is still very high, even if you find that most of it is now pushed in the direction of the affection you show for those around you. Leos who have been looking for romance should not be disappointed now.

27 SUNDAY
Moon Age Day 1 • Moon Sign Virgo

am ....

pm ....

You have a great capacity for hard work and for making up your own mind about things, freed from some of the constrictions that aspects of the day impose upon you. It may be necessary to think about an alteration to the routines that stand before you in the week to come, and to make the necessary arrangements now.

← NEGATIVE TREND							POSITIVE TREND →			
-5	-4	-3	-2	-1		+1	+2	+3	+4	+5
					LOVE					
					MONEY					
					LUCK					
					VITALITY					

28 MONDAY   *Moon Age Day 2 • Moon Sign Virgo*

am ....

pm ....

Travel and appointments generally keep you busy and occupied in the days to come. The start of the working week stimulates a sense of enterprise and allows you to look ahead with a greater sense of optimism than seems to have been the case for a while. There is plenty to be done regarding the practical aspects of life.

29 TUESDAY   *Moon Age Day 3 • Moon Sign Libra*

am ....

pm ....

The hectic pace is still with you and finding all the energy you need to keep things going is not always going to be especially easy. Useful news that comes your way is worth a second look and you discover that there is more to think about than you may have considered.

30 WEDNESDAY   *Moon Age Day 4 • Moon Sign Libra*

am ....

pm ....

Your assertiveness and the strong views that you have on life can be something of a puzzle to others. Confine your interests to those areas of life through which you know successes are possible and don't allow yourself to be held back by the negative options of those around you. Definitely a time to be pleasing yourself.

31 THURSDAY   *Moon Age Day 5 • Moon Sign Scorpio*

am ....

pm ....

You need to feel as close to loved ones as proves to be possible, and this might mean having to talk about deeply personal matters more than would often be the case. A pleasant atmosphere is easy to create, but do beware of pushing any issue more than you know to be sensible or fair. Confidence is not as high as you might wish.

1 FRIDAY

Moon Age Day 6 • Moon Sign Scorpio

am ....

pm ....

Although you are able to manipulate certain situations, it is not at all certain that you will choose to do so. You can sometimes use others in a way that is not all that sensible and may decide that it would be best to leave them to their own devices in the main. A change from the expected patterns of life would be good.

2 SATURDAY

Moon Age Day 7 • Moon Sign Sagittarius

am ....

pm ....

The emphasis is on luxury and pleasure pursuits of one sort or another and the arrival of the weekend allows you to spend just a little more time on such matters. Confusions regarding your personal life should soon be sorted out, though not before you have had a good chat with the people you are closest to.

3 SUNDAY

Moon Age Day 8 • Moon Sign Sagittarius

am ....

pm ....

You may turn out to be rather more assertive than those around you are expecting you to be and this leads to the feeling on their part that you are being bossy. It is very important to explain yourself and to allow some sort of dialogue to take place in both directions. Tact is the most important commodity.

← *NEGATIVE TREND*								*POSITIVE TREND* →		
-5	-4	-3	-2	-1		+1	+2	+3	+4	+5
					LOVE					
					MONEY					
					LUCK					
					VITALITY					

1995

YOUR MONTH AT A GLANCE

The twelve numbered boxes represent the important areas in your life. The key to the numbers you will find beneath the panel. A Sun above the number indicates that opportunities are around. A Cloud below the number, that you should be a bit defensive. Nothing above or below and life will be pretty ordinary.

SEPTEMBER HIGHS AND LOWS

Here, I show how the rhythm of the Moon will affect you this month. Like the tide, your energies and abilities will rise and fall with its pattern. When it is above the date line, go-for-it. When it is below the line you should be resting.

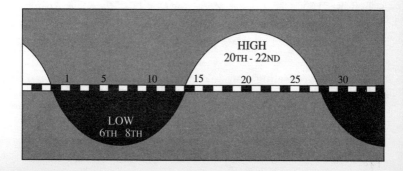

4 MONDAY

Moon Age Day 9 • Moon Sign Capricorn

am ....

pm ....

Social and romantic affairs are very close to your heart as the new working week comes along. Not all the attitudes that you come across are exactly easy to understand and there are occasions when you will have to work very hard even to know what it is that even those close to you are talking about.

5 TUESDAY

Moon Age Day 10 • Moon Sign Capricorn

am ....

pm ....

Establishing a pattern of patient cooperation with loves ones, as well as the people you are working with, is not at all easy at the start of today. However, you should soon settle into a routine and will be anxious to speak your mind. The trouble is that some of the things you have to say are not too popular.

6 WEDNESDAY

Moon Age Day 11 • Moon Sign Aquarius

am ....

pm ....

Snags could develop, and these serve to hold you back at a time when you could really do with getting on more. Being patient with others is not hard, though understanding yourself just isn't too easy at present. Friends and relatives alike are inclined to turn to you for some important help and advice.

7 THURSDAY

Moon Age Day 12 • Moon Sign Aquarius

am ....

pm ....

Although you are feeling more in charge of your daily life, it has to be said that your judgement may not be all you would wish it to be. General energy and enthusiasm is in short supply, and it may be predominantly down to this fact that you can put any hold-ups that do occur. Reasoned argument works best right now.

8 FRIDAY

Moon Age Day 13 • Moon Sign Aquarius

am ....

pm ....

The domestic area of your life is very busy as the working week draws to a close and you may already be deciding exactly what you are going to do with yourself during the weekend. Keeping to chosen paths in a career or practical sense might not be too easy, though there is no real reason for doing so.

9 SATURDAY

Moon Age Day 14 • Moon Sign Pisces

am ....

pm ....

Monetary limits are placed upon you, so there might not be amount of cash around right now that you would wish. Someone in the know could let you in on a secret that turns out to be important with regard to your own life and it is all you can do not to spread the fact around. Relatives understand your thinking.

10 SUNDAY

Moon Age Day 15 • Moon Sign Pisces

am ....

pm ....

Opt for a change of pace regarding social issues, some of which are unlikely to work out to your entire satisfaction. Sunday brings an altered perspective regarding some family matters and you will want to discuss all manner of subjects with people who seem to have your best interests at heart. A warmer personal atmosphere can be expected.

← *NEGATIVE TREND*   *POSITIVE TREND* →

-5	-4	-3	-2	-1		+1	+2	+3	+4	+5
					LOVE					
					MONEY					
					LUCK					
					VITALITY					

11 MONDAY
Moon Age Day 16 • Moon Sign Aries

am ....

pm ....

You could be the source of some gossip today and should stay away from a situation that means you are being involved in any yourself. It doesn't matter how much you deny certain facts, there are people around who simply do not want to know what the truth really is. Light conversation is best, and with those you trust.

12 TUESDAY
Moon Age Day 17 • Moon Sign Aries

am ....

pm ....

A more keen and ambitious approach to life is now obvious, not only to yourself but to almost everyone you are associated with. Certain demands are being made of you but you have the ability to come up with the goods and to make yourself the centre of attention. Not a period when you would want to be on your own too much.

13 WEDNESDAY
Moon Age Day 18 • Moon Sign Taurus

am ....

pm ....

Being as adaptable to changes as you certainly are, you tend to take such situations in your stride. There are a variety of different ways in which you can find yourself making progress and some of them are as a result of the good ideas that come from the direction of friends. It is worth keeping your eyes and ears open.

14 THURSDAY
Moon Age Day 19 • Moon Sign Taurus

am ....

pm ....

You may be forced to toe the line over issues that in reality you feel quite strongly about. Not everyone is on your side at the moment, mainly because they do not really understand what it is that makes you tick. Confining your efforts to a particular area of life is not easy, but may be necessary if you really want to progress.

15 FRIDAY
Moon Age Day 20 • Moon Sign Gemini

am ....

pm ....

You need to feel as if you are part of the gang and so will be mixing as freely with others as turns out to be possible. Some extra rest is necessary if you know that you have been burning the candle at both ends and you could do without pushing yourself so hard at work that you have no energy left to enjoy yourself.

16 SATURDAY
Moon Age Day 21 • Moon Sign Gemini

am ....

pm ....

You show a natural tendency at present to see only the positive side of other people's natures, which may not turn out to be entirely a bad thing, since these self and same people are the ones who can be of the most use to you right now. Nervous energy is going in all directions, but you manage to get a great deal done.

17 SUNDAY
Moon Age Day 22 • Moon Sign Gemini

am ....

pm ....

Time spend on your own today is certainly not at all wasted. There is plenty to do, but you get through any task much easier if you are in a position to please yourself about how you go about doing it. Of course this attitude may not agree with everyone and there may be some explaining to do at some stage.

← *NEGATIVE TREND*   *POSITIVE TREND* →

-5	-4	-3	-2	-1			+1	+2	+3	+4	+5
					LOVE						
					MONEY						
					LUCK						
					VITALITY						

18 MONDAY
Moon Age Day 23 • Moon Sign Cancer

am ....

pm ....

With just a touch of that Leo temper on display tomorrow, there are times when it proves necessary to bite your tongue and keep your opinions to yourself. The best way of all to proceed is to simply refuse to be involved in any sort of argument that you stand no chance of winning. Once again your prefer your own company.

19 TUESDAY
Moon Age Day 24 • Moon Sign Cancer

am ....

pm ....

Unexpected bonuses are likely in a financial sense and some of them could come like a bolt from the blue. In practical matters you are on automatic pilot and will try to assist yourself by only dealing with one job at once. You now show a natural tendency to fight shy of situations that you know to be uncomfortable.

20 WEDNESDAY
Moon Age Day 25 • Moon Sign Leo

am ....

pm ....

Your mind is working so well now that you could genuinely consider this period to be one where you have reached a mental peak. Putting your opinions forward is child's play, even if not everyone appears to have your best interests at heart. Long-term planning is possible and also has a bearing on the immediate future.

21 THURSDAY
Moon Age Day 26 • Moon Sign Leo

am ....

pm ....

An employer or some kind of official could be in a position to do you a real favour and you are in the market for listening to just about anything that may benefit you in the end. Don't be reluctant to speak your mind, though some tact is necessary when you are dealing with people who you know can be over sensitive.

22 FRIDAY
Moon Age Day 27 • Moon Sign Leo

am ....

pm ....

There are snags about when it comes to travel arrangements or appointments of one sort or another. Keep such situations to a minimum, prefering as you do now to stay more or less in the same place. Excitement is possible later in a social sense, though not before you have dealt with the drudgery of the day.

23 SATURDAY
Moon Age Day 28 • Moon Sign Virgo

am ....

pm ....

Your social life is definitely on the up and you have all the energy and determination necessary to get the maximum out of almost anything that is on offer. The small and apparently insignificant details of life carry their own importance as you strive to deal with situations from the past and drive them on to the future.

24 SUNDAY
Moon Age Day 0 • Moon Sign Virgo

am ....

pm ....

You may have to think twice before you decide to spend any money today, mainly because you are inclined to be too lavish, or to find yourself involved in some sort of transaction that will not suit you in the longer term. Active and enterprising later, the end of the day probably suits you much better than its start.

← *NEGATIVE TREND*   *POSITIVE TREND* →

-5	-4	-3	-2	-1		+1	+2	+3	+4	+5
					LOVE					
					MONEY					
					LUCK					
					VITALITY					

25 MONDAY

Moon Age Day 1 • Moon Sign Libra

am ....

pm ....

What at first may seem to be the sort of day that is committed to thoughts about your family and home, later turns out to be a time when you are much more assertive an practical ways. There is a possibility that much more is being asked of you in a workaday sense and no lack of effort on your part to follow through.

26 TUESDAY

Moon Age Day 2 • Moon Sign Libra

am ....

pm ....

You like to appear well informed and to make the most of any opportunity for advancement that comes your way. The problem is that you may not be quite as much in the know as you want to believe and might want to leave some important decision making until a later date. Some Leos could be especially stubborn now.

27 WEDNESDAY

Moon Age Day 3 • Moon Sign Scorpio

am ....

pm ....

Though certain domestic issues tend to be a little irksome, and probably very inconvenient, you will have to get them sorted out before you start to push forward with more personal plans. If this means committing most of the day towards house and home, at least later you will have that much more time to please yourself.

28 THURSDAY

Moon Age Day 4 • Moon Sign Scorpio

am ....

pm ....

Useful input from all sorts of directions is now likely to come your way, and it does so at just the right time. There is no piece of information too small for you to take account of it, or its implications. It is a fact that you see practical openings which others have failed to recognise at this time.

29 FRIDAY
Moon Age Day 5 • Moon Sign Sagittarius

am ....

pm ....

You now fight shy of situations that you automatically do not care for the look of, and this is probably no bad thing at the end of a busy and sometimes even exhausting working week. The simple fact is that you have probably being doing far more than has been good for you and now genuinely need a well earned rest.

30 SATURDAY
Moon Age Day 6 • Moon Sign Sagittarius

am ....

pm ....

Romance and all aspects of pleasure allow you the leeway to think and act in the way that you wish to exclusively. Confidence to do the right thing at the right time is going out through the roof and most people are left in little or no doubt as to how your mind is presently working. You have a good ability to concentrate.

1 SUNDAY
Moon Age Day 7 • Moon Sign Sagittarius

am ....

pm ....

Work issues are not too much of a problem today, though there are people about who do not really want to deal with such matters on a Sunday. Just because you are in the mood to look and plan ahead does not mean that everyone you come across is in a similar frame of mind. Some fresh air and a little exercise might do you good.

← *NEGATIVE TREND*						*POSITIVE TREND* →				
-5	-4	-3	-2	-1		+1	+2	+3	+4	+5
					LOVE					
					MONEY					
					LUCK					
					VITALITY					

1995

YOUR MONTH AT A GLANCE

The twelve numbered boxes represent the important areas in your life. The key to the numbers you will find beneath the panel. A Sun above the number indicates that opportunities are around. A Cloud below the number, that you should be a bit defensive. Nothing above or below and life will be pretty ordinary.

1	2	3	4	5 ☀	6	7	8 ☀	9 ☀	10	11	12
					☁	☁					

KEY

1 Strength of Personality
2 Personal Finance
3 Useful Information Gathering
4 Domestic Affairs
5 Pleasure & Romance
6 Effective Work & Health

7 One to One Relationships
8 Questioning, Thinking & Deciding
9 External Influences / Education
10 Career Aspirations
11 Teamwork Activities
12 Unconscious Impulses

OCTOBER HIGHS AND LOWS

Here, I show how the rhythm of the Moon will affect you this month. Like the tide, your energies and abilities will rise and fall with its pattern. When it is above the date line, go-for-it. When it is below the line you should be resting.

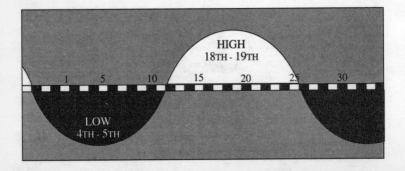

2 MONDAY
Moon Age Day 8 • Moon Sign Capricorn

am ....

pm ....

You could find that you are receiving a boost from the sort of changes that are taking place around your homestead at this time and will want to set your house in order for a number of different reasons. Carrying on with the same old routines that have been part of your life for a while could seem a drag.

3 TUESDAY
Moon Age Day 9 • Moon Sign Capricorn

am ....

pm ....

Financial problems are not exactly inevitable today, though they are a distinct possibility and one that you should be aware of at all stages. Concern for others is growing, and especially so in a family sense. A creative and inspiring period is at hand and you will want to do what you can to feed your own need for variety.

4 WEDNESDAY
Moon Age Day 10 • Moon Sign Aqaurius

am ....

pm ....

Let your partner or a good friend handle those situations that you do not care for the look of personally, that way you free more time to please yourself and to do the sort of things that captivate your own imagination. What you can do without at present is trying to or- ganise the lives of everyone else.

5 THURSDAY
Moon Age Day 11 • Moon Sign Aqaurius

am ....

pm ....

There may be a very rewarding period showing itself now, and you really are in the right mood to take on the world and win. Of course, not everyone is going to be on your side all the time and the at- titudes of friends are somewhat difficult to understand on occasion. Keep to tried and tested paths when dealing with relatives.

6 FRIDAY
Moon Age Day 12 • Moon Sign Pisces

am ....

pm ....

Socially speaking you present a charming face to the world and will be doing everything within your power to stay out there in the mainstream of life, having a good time and making as much of all possibilities as you realistically can. You might have some rather difficult news to impart and must remain tactful.

7 SATURDAY
Moon Age Day 13 • Moon Sign Pisces

am ....

pm ....

The way others are talking today could lead you to believe that they do not really have your best interests at heart, something that is going to be a little difficult for you to come to terms with. Still, as long as you are in a position to monitor the fact, all should be well. Try to remain generally optimistic.

8 SUNDAY
Moon Age Day 14 • Moon Sign Aries

am ....

pm ....

You can take a few liberties at present, knowing that you are in the best position of all to get away with almost anything. There is a generally carefree approach to life that you find refreshing and useful. Sorting out the life of a close friend may be slightly more difficult than dealing with your own however.

← NEGATIVE TREND						POSITIVE TREND →				
-5	-4	-3	-2	-1		+1	+2	+3	+4	+5
					LOVE					
					MONEY					
					LUCK					
					VITALITY					

9 MONDAY
Moon Age Day 15 • Moon Sign Aries

am ....

pm ....

There are plenty of people around right now who would be more than willing to gain the upper hand if you were to allow them to do so. Confining yourself to those subjects that you know and understand just for the moment might be best, especially since you are not really quite as efficient as you sometimes are.

10 TUESDAY
Moon Age Day 16 • Moon Sign Taurus

am ....

pm ....

A softening effect of certain aspects of life is now in evidence, so much so that you want to do everything within your power to show that you are on the side of relatives, not all of whom are behaving is quite the way that you might expect. This should be an excellent time domestically, with forward planning a must.

11 WEDNESDAY
Moon Age Day 17 • Moon Sign Taurus

am ....

pm ....

Professional situations bring the sort of strains to bear on your that you could certainly do without just now, though nothing that you would find all that difficult to deal with if you only take some time out to think about things. An attitude problem is something that friends tend to show at first today.

12 THURSDAY
Moon Age Day 18 • Moon Sign Taurus

am ....

pm ....

People from the past now return to the fold and may inspire you by their example and the way that they have altered their own lives. As far as you are concerned this is likely to give good food for thought and creates a situation which you are able to deal with in a sensible and typically Leonine fashion.

13 FRIDAY
Moon Age Day 19 • Moon Sign Gemini

am ....

pm ....

Others want to challenge your ideas and opinions all the time now and there is nothing else for it but to go along with what is being expected of you. Trying not to argue is something that you find more than a little difficult and gives you something of a special problem in a professional sense at some stage tomorrow.

14 SATURDAY
Moon Age Day 20 • Moon Sign Gemini

am ....

pm ....

Congenial and friendly surroundings are your lot today and the weekend offers a number of diversions that you may not have been expecting. Concern for those who are not as well off as you are can be part of your thinking and this is a time when you are quite willing to put yourself out on behalf of others.

15 SUNDAY
Moon Age Day 21 • Moon Sign Cancer

am ....

pm ....

Minor improvements and changes to your living accommodation, or to the general circumstances immediately surrounding your home may well be one of the factors that you are looking at closely just at present. Creating a good atmosphere for loved ones is also on your mind, particularly as there is more time to talk to them.

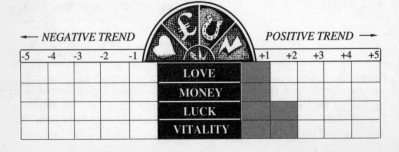

← NEGATIVE TREND								POSITIVE TREND →				
-5	-4	-3	-2	-1				+1	+2	+3	+4	+5
					LOVE							
					MONEY							
					LUCK							
					VITALITY							

16 MONDAY
Moon Age Day 22 • Moon Sign Cancer

am ....

pm ....

You might prefer to remain in the shadows more than would usually be the case for your gregarious sign. Finding the privacy that you are seeking could turn out to be far less likely than you imagine, and so some minor frustrations are likely to emerge as a result. Others tend to demand your attention more than you would wish.

17 TUESDAY
Moon Age Day 23 • Moon Sign Cancer

am ....

pm ....

What a very important time this is for making decisions of almost any sort, and in the certain knowledge that you have the power to get things right. Someone you haven't seen for ages comes back on the scene, bringing with them all sorts of ideas that are going to be useful when it comes to sorting out your own future.

18 WEDNESDAY
Moon Age Day 24 • Moon Sign Leo

am ....

pm ....

Although you are a little reluctant to ask favours from people who you know to have influence and even power, there is no doubt at all that this is the time for you to be doing so. An active period is promised, with much in the way of change and diversity of those of you who are willing to make certain, small sacrifices.

19 THURSDAY
Moon Age Day 25 • Moon Sign Leo

am ....

pm ....

There may be some unexpected conflict now brewing in or around your home, and though you may not be the one who is starting the situation, it could easily be left up to you to sort it out in the end. Don't submit to the will of others on those occasions when you know that you own point of view is the right one.

20 FRIDAY
Moon Age Day 26 • Moon Sign Virgo

am ....

pm ....

Romance and pleasure pursuits of all sorts now form the basis upon which you are thinking and acting. Conforming the suspicions of people who think they understand the way your mind works might prove to be a little annoying personally, but in the end puts them in a position to do you more for you.

21 SATURDAY
Moon Age Day 27 • Moon Sign Virgo

am ....

pm ....

This is not a time for allowing others to talk you out of things that you know are good for you, and since your relationships with those around you are more complicated this week than may have seemed to be the case for quite some time, you do need to be especially careful. Confidence is lacking concerning some issues.

22 SUNDAY
Moon Age Day 28 • Moon Sign Virgo

am ....

pm ....

Though personal plans and objectives work out to your complete satisfaction as Sunday settles upon you, it might be difficult to make the sort of concrete progress that you are really looking for. Someone in the know, probably within the family, has some interesting news to impart, so it's worth taking time out to listen.

NEGATIVE TREND							POSITIVE TREND			
-5	-4	-3	-2	-1			+1	+2	+3	+4	+5
					LOVE						
					MONEY						
					LUCK						
					VITALITY						

23 MONDAY   *Moon Age Day 0 • Moon Sign Libra*

am ....

pm ....

Your ego is very high at the start of this working week, and as a result you do need to be certain that you are not putting more pressure on others than you really intend to do. Much of your energy goes towards making your own working and living conditions more comfortable, a fact that can also have a positive bearing on relatives.

24 TUESDAY   *Moon Age Day 1 • Moon Sign Libra*

am ....

pm ....

With the sun now entering your solar fourth house, you should find a period of emotional stability settling in for a month or so. This allows you to make any small changes at home that you have been thinking about and could also open up a period when you find relatives somewhat easier to deal with in a general sense.

25 WEDNESDAY   *Moon Age Day 2 • Moon Sign Scorpio*

am ....

pm ....

Expert advice is coming in from someone who is clearly in the know and this is something that you would not want to turn away, at least not without looking at it very carefully. A short journey could have a very positive part to play in your thinking at some stage today, if you can find the time to contemplate it.

26 THURSDAY   *Moon Age Day 3 • Moon Sign Scorpio*

am ....

pm ....

You seem to need to the approval of more than one person before you embark on situations that you know to be important. It isn't that you lack the determination to make decisions of your own, but you see the sense in being willing to look at things from a different sort of perspective. Hesitation is a possibility.

27 FRIDAY
Moon Age Day 4 • Moon Sign Sagittarius

am ....

pm ....

Your protective instincts are inclined to be aroused more than you might wish, and as a result you do what you can to look after family members and friends alike. This is a period when the bravery and supportive qualities of your sign are really showing out, and during which you can make much of even small opportunities.

28 SATURDAY
Moon Age Day 5 • Moon Sign Sagittarius

am ....

pm ....

The atmosphere at home today is so warm and comfortable that you can make the weekend your own. Ideas come in thick and fast, and not all of them out of your own head either. Trying out new ideas could be one of your chosen tasks for the weekend, but do your best to make certain that others are taken into your confidence.

29 SUNDAY
Moon Age Day 6 • Moon Sign Capricorn

am ....

pm ....

The wheels of progress turn more swiftly than you might imagine, despite the fact that the arrival of Sunday also offers something in the way of relaxation for Leos who are feeling a little lazy. Creating space for yourself at home means having to come to terms with relatives, some of whom are reticent to allow changes.

← NEGATIVE TREND						POSITIVE TREND →				
-5	-4	-3	-2	-1		+1	+2	+3	+4	+5
					LOVE					
					MONEY					
					LUCK					
					VITALITY					

30 MONDAY
Moon Age Day 7 • Moon Sign Capricorn

am ....

pm ....

At the start of a new working week there is little doubt that there are delays in the offing. Going around with a smile on your face, no matter what seems to be going wrong, would be a distinct advantage at present, and someone who notices the fact will put themselves in a position to be of great assistance.

31 TUESDAY
Moon Age Day 8 • Moon Sign Aquarius

am ....

pm ....

Keep yourself to yourself whenever it proves to be possible to do so at present. You really are not in the right mood to be mixing as freely as would usually be the case and the power of the moon to slow your life down is especially noticeable at present. Consideration for others tends to come as second nature now.

1 WEDNESDAY
Moon Age Day 9 • Moon Sign Aquarius

am ....

pm ....

There may be a tendency to look on the blacker side of life just for the moment, and there is no doubt that this is something that you really should avoid doing if at all possible. Work on slowly and steadily towards your chosen objectives and don't allow yourself to be held back by the negative attitudes of friends.

2 THURSDAY
Moon Age Day 10 • Moon Sign Pisces

am ....

pm ....

A loved one or a family member may be throwing his or her weight about more than you think is sensible today, so that biting your lip is not at all easy. Reacting to any situation is worth thinking about before you do it, since you can cause all sorts of potential problems for yourself if you are not very careful.

3 FRIDAY

Moon Age Day 11 • Moon Sign Pisces

am ....

pm ....

It looks as though romance is in the air in a big way for you. A new period commences when you are definitely showing the sort of popularity in company of which you are quite capable. There are gains to be made as a result, many of which have a much further-reaching aspect than might appear to be the case at first.

4 SATURDAY

Moon Age Day 12 • Moon Sign Aries

am ....

pm ....

A change of scenery would suit you down to the ground, and so this is what you are likely to be looking for at some stage today. Not everyone is running as true to form as you might expect them to and as a result you need to keep your eyes and ears open, monitoring any situation that you can.

5 SUNDAY

Moon Age Day 13 • Moon Sign Aries

am ....

pm ....

You have a good flair for expressing yourself in positive terms, not that this means you can bring everyone round to a point of view that you know to be fair and reasonable. You look on the bright side of life today however and can be on the receiving end of compliments that come from a host of different directions.

← *NEGATIVE TREND*   *POSITIVE TREND* →

-5	-4	-3	-2	-1			+1	+2	+3	+4	+5
					LOVE						
					MONEY						
					LUCK						
					VITALITY						

1995

YOUR MONTH AT A GLANCE

The twelve numbered boxes represent the important areas in your life.
The key to the numbers you will find beneath the panel. A Sun above
the number indicates that opportunities are around. A Cloud below
the number, that you should be a bit defensive. Nothing above or
below and life will be pretty ordinary.

| 1 | 2 | 3 | 4 | 5 | 6 | 7 | 8 | 9 | 10 | 11 | 12 |

KEY

1 Strength of Personality	7 One to One Relationships
2 Personal Finance	8 Questioning, Thinking & Deciding
3 Useful Information Gathering	9 External Influences / Education
4 Domestic Affairs	10 Career Aspirations
5 Pleasure & Romance	11 Teamwork Activities
6 Effective Work & Health	12 Unconscious Impulses

NOVEMBER HIGHS AND LOWS

Here, I show how the rhythm of the Moon will affect you this month.
Like the tide, your energies and abilities will rise and fall with its pattern. When it is above the date line, go-for-it. When it is below the
line you should be resting.

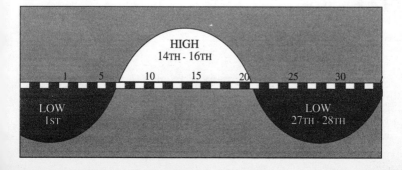

HIGH
14TH - 16TH

LOW
1ST

LOW
27TH - 28TH

6 MONDAY
Moon Age Day 14 • Moon Sign Aries

am ....

pm ....

Discussions relating to family matters are clearly important now and
you should take some time out at some stage during the day to sort
them out. In a more professional sense you are anxious to do what
you can to make life happy for all sorts of people in your circle and
you will be seeking ways to improve your personal life.

7 TUESDAY
Moon Age Day 15 • Moon Sign Taurus

am ....

pm ....

Continued reliance on your colleagues could get you down a little at
work, especially if the people concerned find means and ways to
make you show your gratitude for the situation. Anxiety is a factor
in your life, even though you are doing your best to keep it to a minimum. Confidence is not especially high on.

8 WEDNESDAY
Moon Age Day 16 • Moon Sign Taurus

am ....

pm ....

You benefit from the sort of help and advice that comes from well-
meaning individuals who enter your life from a host of different
directions. Someone who you know to be particularly useful in helping you to order your future is close to you throughout the remainder
of this week, so use their influence.

9 THURSDAY
Moon Age Day 17 • Moon Sign Gemini

am ....

pm ....

You certainly prefer the company of friends to that of people who
have not played a particularly important part in your life of late.
Significant alterations to your schedules may be necessary if you are
to get as much out of life as you might hope right now. Any sort of
anxiety is to be avoided at all cost.

10 FRIDAY

Moon Age Day 18 • Moon Sign Gemini

am ....

pm ....

Strong words are likely to be exchanged between yourself and someone who you have never really seen eye to eye with in the past. There is no shortage of work to be done, the only problem being that you may not have the time to get it all out of the way before the weekend comes along. Consideration is all-important.

11 SATURDAY

Moon Age Day 19 • Moon Sign Gemini

am ....

pm ....

You could be rather prone to listening too much to what others have to say, a factor that prevents you from making up your own mind quite to the extent that you might. A sound proposal coming from someone within the family deserves more than a cursory glance and there should be time today to talk sensibly about things.

12 SUNDAY

Moon Age Day 20 • Moon Sign Cancer

am ....

pm ....

Issues at home, in some way related to your family, take time to deal with, probably preventing you from making as much of the day as would otherwise be the case. Certain people who are close to you have compliments to pay you, which make you feel very much better about yourself than has possibly been possible for a while.

← NEGATIVE TREND						POSITIVE TREND →				
-5	-4	-3	-2	-1		+1	+2	+3	+4	+5
					LOVE					
					MONEY					
					LUCK					
					VITALITY					

13 MONDAY

Moon Age Day 21 • Moon Sign Cancer

am ....

pm ....

Your personality shines out as strongly as a beacon now, which means you start the working week showing more in the way of confidence than might have been possible for quite a while. Those you rely on are difficult to deal with on occasions, but you have ways and means to get your own way with them at present.

14 TUESDAY

Moon Age Day 22 • Moon Sign Leo

am ....

pm ....

Everyday matters are easy to deal with and offer you the incentive that you need to plan the remainder of the week, free from fetters of convention. The desire to be yourself and to do whatever takes your fancy is obvious, not only to you, but also to the people you are dealing with in your working and social life.

15 WEDNESDAY

Moon Age Day 23 • Moon Sign Leo

am ....

pm ....

Put your powers of persuasion to the test. There is really very little that you cannot achieve right now, simply by being willing to speak your mind. The more creative aspects of your nature allow you to make gains that only a few days ago might well have seemed to be out of the question. Don't hold back in romantic matters.

16 THURSDAY

Moon Age Day 24 • Moon Sign Leo

am ....

pm ....

Certain practical considerations require more in the way of attention and stamina now and you have all the energy at your disposal that could possibly need in order to see your life following chosen paths. Your instincts are honed to perfection, allowing you to react to your hunches with some hope of success.

170

17 FRIDAY

Moon Age Day 25 • Moon Sign Virgo

am ....

pm ....

Be careful that you do not find yourself in the position of blaming others for things that you know are your own fault. When things do go wrong, it would be sensible to stand back from them and look at all situations carefully, probably taking on some advice from those of your friends who you know to be especially wise.

18 SATURDAY

Moon Age Day 26 • Moon Sign Virgo

am ....

pm ....

Keep abreast of vital news, at least for the moment. You can't really help yourself all that much if you stay in the house and refuse to mix with those individuals who are in the know. Although you show an urge to do whatever takes your fancy personally, at least part of the day needs to be socially motivated.

19 SUNDAY

Moon Age Day 27 • Moon Sign Libra

am ....

pm ....

A family member ought to be in a position to do you a significant favour today, and it's one that puts you in a good position when it comes to looking at the possibilities of the new working week ahead of you. Do your best to make certain that there are least some moments during which you can please yourself romantically.

← NEGATIVE TREND							POSITIVE TREND →			
-5	-4	-3	-2	-1			+1	+2	+3	+4	+5
				LOVE						
				MONEY						
			LUCK							
				VITALITY						

20 MONDAY
Moon Age Day 28 • Moon Sign Libra

am ....

pm ....

The present position of the planet Venus stimulates the more
romantic elements of your nature, making it possible for you to find
gains within close personal relationships. You draw much in the
way of assistance from members of the opposite sex, not to mention
the personal satisfaction that comes from your popularity.

21 TUESDAY
Moon Age Day 29 • Moon Sign Scorpio

am ....

pm ....

Important professional matters should not be overlooked, something
that would be all too easy to do right now. In your desire to make
life work out as you would wish in other spheres you are inclined to
miss the wood for the trees. A friend could be seeking your assistance concerning a matter that is not working out for them.

22 WEDNESDAY
Moon Age Day 0 • Moon Sign Scorpio

am ....

pm ....

Another important boost to your personal and romantic life can now
be expected. Earlier in the month, romance was important for its
own sake, though now there is a chance that its implications spill
over into other areas of your life too. New incentives at work look
especially good, with possible advancement on offer.

23 THURSDAY
Moon Age Day 1 • Moon Sign Sagittarius

am ....

pm ....

A recently formed friendship shows the chance of developing into
something much more if you are willing to put the effort into it at
present. You tend to attract the goodwill of almost everyone who
plays a part in your life, even if there are occasions when you have to
be willing to go out and look for it directly.

24 FRIDAY

Moon Age Day 2 • Moon Sign Sagittarius

am ....

pm ....

You seem prepared to go to almost any lengths to get what you want from life today, and as this is the end of the working week for most of you, a sudden burst of energy might not turn out to be a bad thing at all. Save some of your reserves for the weekend ahead however, as there are strong social impulses coming.

25 SATURDAY

Moon Age Day 3 • Moon Sign Capricorn

am ....

pm ....

Certain matters leave you cold, even though you know in your heart of hearts that you should be putting in the maximum amount of effort in order to get ahead generally right now. Something that you want in a personal sense is certainly worth fighting for, but there are many ways and means of doing so.

26 SUNDAY

Moon Age Day 4 • Moon Sign Capricorn

am ....

pm ....

Working in any way in cooperation with others clearly suits you the best at the present time, even though there are some types about who are not half as helpful as you might be expecting. Your level of give and take are excellent, but the same cannot be said for those closest to you, who are probably feeling grumpy.

← *NEGATIVE TREND*   *POSITIVE TREND* →

	-5	-4	-3	-2	-1		+1	+2	+3	+4	+5
LOVE				▓							
MONEY					▓						
LUCK							▓	▓	▓		
VITALITY								▓			

27 MONDAY
Moon Age Day 5 • Moon Sign Aquarius

am ....

pm ....

It might be best to take a calm and unstressed view of the world at large today, if it proves possible to do so. This is a time for regrouping with others and for conserving your energy, which is not especially strong at present. The least effort you have to put into anything, the better you find life is working out.

28 TUESDAY
Moon Age Day 6 • Moon Sign Aquarius

am ....

pm ....

Personal setbacks are something of a possibility, and you have to work harder than usual to get what you want from the day as a whole. This should not be especially difficult, bearing in mind your sign and the amount of get up and go which is always evident within you. An active period at home is likely later in the day.

29 WEDNESDAY
Moon Age Day 7 • Moon Sign Pisces

am ....

pm ....

Your motivations for getting on with things are strictly personal at present and it is fair to say that you will not take particularly kindly to others telling you how you should behave during the middle of this week. Confrontations should be kept to a minimum however, and not allowed to interfere with your progress.

30 THURSDAY
Moon Age Day 8 • Moon Sign Pisces

am ....

pm ....

A new period of energy comes to your aid, lifting your spirits and making it more likely that you will be looking ahead towards a brighter and more successful sort of future. Creative energy shines out like a star, allowing you to give some time to projects that may be of no material benefit but which suit you personally, simply because you are feeling like undertaking them.

1 FRIDAY

Moon Age Day 9 • Moon Sign Pisces

am ....

pm ....

The bright lights of social world now tend to beckon you, so don't be distracted from professional obligations simply on their account. All the same, you do need to enjoy yourself sometimes, and with the weekend ahead of you, why not get your thinking cap on now? What you really need is a change of scenery.

2 SATURDAY

Moon Age Day 10 • Moon Sign Aries

am ....

pm ....

Practical matters are now virtually a labour of love, and you whisk around your abode with a desire to sort things out in a way that you have clearly avoided doing in the past. Some new friends can be made at this time and you also have the ability to turn the heads of strangers, even those of a very different nature.

3 SUNDAY

Moon Age Day 11 • Moon Sign Aries

am ....

pm ....

Beware of adopting the sort of attitude towards others that you know will only make a heated situation that much worse. You can deflect trouble, simply by ensuring that you are in the right place at the right time. Give and take turn out to be especially important in personal relationships, and in your dealings with some friends.

← NEGATIVE TREND   *POSITIVE TREND →*

-5	-4	-3	-2	-1			+1	+2	+3	+4	+5
					LOVE						
					MONEY						
					LUCK						
					VITALITY						

1995
YOUR MONTH AT A GLANCE

The twelve numbered boxes represent the important areas in your life. The key to the numbers you will find beneath the panel. A Sun above the number indicates that opportunities are around. A Cloud below the number, that you should be a bit defensive. Nothing above or below and life will be pretty ordinary.

			☀	☀		☀					
1	2	3	4	5	6	7	8	9	10	11	12
	☁										

KEY

1 Strength of Personality
2 Personal Finance
3 Useful Information Gathering
4 Domestic Affairs
5 Pleasure & Romance
6 Effective Work & Health

7 One to One Relationships
8 Questioning, Thinking & Deciding
9 External Influences / Education
10 Career Aspirations
11 Teamwork Activities
12 Unconscious Impulses

DECEMBER HIGHS AND LOWS

Here, I show how the rhythm of the Moon will affect you this month. Like the tide, your energies and abilities will rise and fall with its pattern. When it is above the date line, go-for-it. When it is below the line you should be resting.

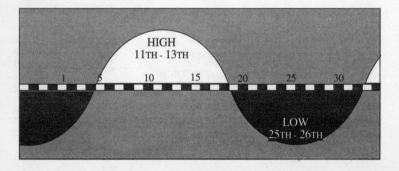

4 MONDAY *Moon Age Day 12 • Moon Sign Taurus*

am ....

pm ....

There may be extra responsibilities about that you do not really care for the look of, though these do have to be dealt with at some stage, even if you really are not in the mood for them. Acting on impulse may not be as easy for you now as would normally be the case, which could be a good thing.

5 TUESDAY *Moon Age Day 13 • Moon Sign Taurus*

am ....

pm ....

The emphasis now is on pressing ahead with matters that you see as being of primary importance to you in the longer term. This would not be a fortunate period for lingering, or for looking back in any way. The more you manage to get yourself facing the implications of a necessary future, the better you feel.

6 WEDNESDAY *Moon Age Day 14 • Moon Sign Gemini*

am ....

pm ....

A friend or a social contact of some kind has some important and quite startling news to impart in the near future. Give yourself a little time to enjoy the social implications of life, freed from the fetters of immediate responsibility, on this, one of the most changeable weeks you are likely to encounter for a while.

7 THURSDAY *Moon Age Day 15 • Moon Sign Gemini*

am ....

pm ....

An excellent time for all matters associated with romance and pleasure pursuits. You need the company of like-minded and interesting people at all stages right now and can gain from the new and interesting ideas that they bring into your life. You can't be as attentive to family members as you may perhaps wish.

8 FRIDAY
Moon Age Day 16 • Moon Sign Gemini

am ....

pm ....

Minor professional difficulties are likely to arise early in the day, though nothing that you should find all that difficult to deal with in the longer term. Deal with any awkward situations one at a time and get your priorities right. There is great kindness shown to you by special friends, who have your interests at heart.

9 SATURDAY
Moon Age Day 17 • Moon Sign Cancer

am ....

pm ....

You are now quite prepared to make whatever concessions prove to be necessary in order to see life working out as you would wish for loved ones. With the weekend ahead you can do whatever it takes to make others happy and should be spending time talking to them. A good interlude for doing whatever you want personally.

10 SUNDAY
Moon Age Day 18 • Moon Sign Cancer

am ....

pm ....

A stronger than usual element of luck now enters your life, allowing you to make one or two gambles that, under normal circumstances, you might be inclined to shy away from. Exceptional circumstances may demand a revolutionary way of looking at life, and you are just the person to do so.

← NEGATIVE TREND								POSITIVE TREND →		
-5	-4	-3	-2	-1			+1	+2	+3	+4	+5
					LOVE						
					MONEY						
					LUCK						
					VITALITY						

11 MONDAY *Moon Age Day 19 • Moon Sign Leo*

am ....

pm ....

All that is required in order to see success coming into your life at the moment is confidence in your own ability and the desire to get ahead. There is a world full of people who will do all that they can to see you getting on and plenty of incentive to lift your own efforts to match the circumstances surrounding you.

12 TUESDAY *Moon Age Day 20 • Moon Sign Leo*

am ....

pm ....

Discussions at work could prove to be very fruitful and can lead you down the path to new ideas of your own that turn out to be especially rewarding in one way or another. You will want to make the most of friendships that come into your life at this time and can find people who are very easy to rely on.

13 WEDNESDAY *Moon Age Day 21 • Moon Sign Leo*

am ....

pm ....

Don't try to mix business with pleasure today because it is a combination that really will not work for you. Keeping the various elements of living apart may not be at all easy, though you should be very grateful in the end that you tried. Advice offered to a friend later in the day could apply to you too.

14 THURSDAY *Moon Age Day 22 • Moon Sign Virgo*

am ....

pm ....

Minor monetary gains are going to find their way to your door in the near future, even if it is slightly doubtful as to whether you personally have much to do with the situation. Confidence to do the right thing appears to be on the increase, not that you are in a position to argue with your present actions in any case.

179

15 FRIDAY
Moon Age Day 23 • Moon Sign Virgo

am ....

pm ....

You may be in too much of a hurry to arrive at your own goals today, and that means that you need to slow things down a little and wait to see how the grass grows in personal sense. It's true that not everyone around you is being all that helpful at the moment, but you have more than enough incentive in any case.

16 SATURDAY
Moon Age Day 24 • Moon Sign Libra

am ....

pm ....

Meetings, schedules and appointments of all kinds have a part to play in the way that you order your weekend. You are casting part of your mind ahead to the festive season and will want to be planning functions of one sort or another before it is too late. Not everyone is quite as helpful with this regard as they might be.

17 SUNDAY
Moon Age Day 25 • Moon Sign Libra

am ....

pm ....

Love issues now put you on a winning streak, and it's one that sees you making progress in a personal sense of a type that may not have been possible earlier in the month. Attitudes vary within the family, but you move on slowly and steadily towards major objectives that have not varied in your mind for some time.

← *NEGATIVE TREND*   *POSITIVE TREND* →

-5	-4	-3	-2	-1			+1	+2	+3	+4	+5
					LOVE						
					MONEY						
					LUCK						
					VITALITY						

18 MONDAY
Moon Age Day 26 • Moon Sign Libra

am ....

pm ....

Domestic demands could prove to be more tiring than you imagine at the start of the new working week, and these take away from you some of the energy which otherwise you would want to put into your working life. This is a period for showing the whole world at large what you are made of and for taking any bull by the horns.

19 TUESDAY
Moon Age Day 27 • Moon Sign Scorpio

am ....

pm ....

Keep track of both professional and personal matters, doing all that you can to make life work to your advantage. It would be too easy to find yourself distracted by the things other people are saying and also by their opinions, which may not be quite as sound as you had hoped. Romance is favoured later in the day.

20 WEDNESDAY
Moon Age Day 28 • Moon Sign Scorpio

am ....

pm ....

Though love issues and pleasure pursuits appear to have an importance and a significance all of their own today, you carry on in your own sweet way towards the practical requirements of a busy period, without worrying too much about the personal distractions that occasionally stand in your way at present.

21 THURSDAY
Moon Age Day 0 • Moon Sign Sagittarius

am ....

pm ....

An excellent period for all one-to-one dealings with others, and especially so when it comes to putting the finishing touches to plans for Christmas. In any sort of battle at work, it looks as though you have almost everyone on your side, not that you will want to force any issue that you can deal with in a diplomatic way.

22 FRIDAY

Moon Age Day 1 • Moon Sign Sagittarius

am ....

pm ....

Excellent results can be achieved by doing what you want, and certainly by not following the advice or seeming instructions of anyone who clearly does not know you at all. A physical peak is achieved, during which you have sufficient energy to do whatever takes your fancy, and without feeling that you are taking too much on.

23 SATURDAY

Moon Age Day 2 • Moon Sign Capricorn

am ....

pm ....

Ego clashes with certain types are more or less inevitable at some stage today, though they can be avoided if you are willing to bite your tongue a little more than you usually would. Of course this is not at all easy for you to do, and you might even have to keep out of the way altogether in order to maintain an impartial standpoint.

24 SUNDAY

Moon Age Day 3 • Moon Sign Capricorn

am ....

pm ....

Despite the impending Christmas celebrations, there are still practical matters on your mind that you will want to deal with at this time. In some ways you could be feeling just a little out of sorts with yourself and will want to do all that you can socially to redress the balance. With friends to help, this should not be difficult.

← NEGATIVE TREND							POSITIVE TREND →			
-5	-4	-3	-2	-1		+1	+2	+3	+4	+5
					LOVE					
					MONEY					
					LUCK					
					VITALITY					

25 MONDAY   *Moon Age Day 4 • Moon Sign Aquarius*

am ....

pm ....

If you focus your attention on the possibilities of a social and family Christmas, you should find today to be just about as positive as anything that you have enjoyed in the past Christmas-wise. There are probably some surprises about that you did not expect and these could be related to people, rather than presents.

26 TUESDAY   *Moon Age Day 5 • Moon Sign Aquarius*

am ....

pm ....

A belated Christmas gift is possible for you today and you should also find this to be an excellent time for getting out and about. A return to old values in one way or another could prove to be very necessary and you will not find that restrictions placed upon you by others alter in any way your capacity to enjoy the day.

27 WEDNESDAY   *Moon Age Day 6 • Moon Sign Pisces*

am ....

pm ....

Close emotional relationships are preferred at this time, and so new friendships do tend to take something of a back seat in your life for the moment. Catering for the needs of your family would appear to be high on your list of priorities and there are some fairly exciting prospects in store, that is if you take note of them.

28 THURSDAY   *Moon Age Day 7 • Moon Sign Pisces*

am ....

pm ....

Out there in the social mainstream of life, you enjoy everything that is on offer, and in the company of people you get on very well with. Routines of any description may have a tendency to bore you however and you will be doing all that you can to stay away from them. Outmoded concepts should be left behind.

29 FRIDAY

Moon Age Day 8 • Moon Sign Aries

am ....

pm ....

One-to-one relationships provide you with all that you need to remain content in the days that lie ahead of you. For the moment you may find that it is still difficult to get yourself into quite the state of mind to fulfil all the practical requirements that you would normally get through with little problem.

30 SATURDAY

Moon Age Day 9 • Moon Sign Aries

am ....

pm ....

Another high-profile day, when you will be doing all that you can to establish your position within the social circles that mean so much to you. With social functions of one sort or another now in the pipeline, you have plenty to keep you occupied and time to spare to do whatever takes your personal fancy.

31 SUNDAY

Moon Age Day 10 • Moon Sign Taurus

am ....

pm ....

You are busy making preparations for an active and positive start to the new year and in some ways this fact shows itself already. With great enthusiasm you look forward to what the day has to offer and should be on the go from the moment you get out of bed until well after Big Ben strikes January into being.

← *NEGATIVE TREND*								*POSITIVE TREND* →			
-5	-4	-3	-2	-1			+1	+2	+3	+4	+5
					LOVE						
					MONEY						
					LUCK						
					VITALITY						

RISING SIGNS
for LEO

Look along the top to find your date of birth, and down the side fo
hour (or two) if appropriate for Summer Time.

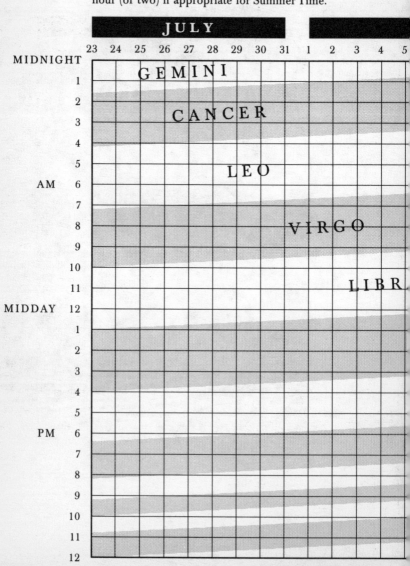

	JULY												
	23	24	25	26	27	28	29	30	31	1	2	3	4	5

MIDNIGHT

GEMINI
CANCER
LEO
VIRGO
LIBR

AM

MIDDAY

PM

birth time. Where they cross is your Rising Sign. Don't forget to subtract an

AUGUST

| 8 | 9 | 10 | 11 | 12 | 13 | 14 | 15 | 16 | 17 | 18 | 19 | 20 | 21 | 22 | 23 |

0
1
2
3
4
5
6
7
8
9
10
11
12
1
2
3
4
5
6
7
8
9
10
11
12

RPIO

SAGITTARIUS

CAPRICORN

AQUARIUS

PISCES

ARIES

TAURUS

GEMINI

THE ZODIAC AT A GLANCE

Placed	Sign	Symbol	Glyph	Polarity	Element	Quality	Planet	Glyph	Metal	Stone	Opposite
1	Aries	Ram	♈	+	Fire	Cardinal	Mars	♂	Iron	Bloodstone	Libra
2	Taurus	Bull	♉	–	Earth	Fixed	Venus	♀	Copper	Sapphire	Scorpio
3	Gemini	Twins	♊	+	Air	Mutable	Mercury	☿	Mercury	Tiger's Eye	Sagittarius
4	Cancer	Crab	♋	–	Water	Cardinal	Moon	☽	Silver	Pearl	Capricorn
5	Leo	Lion	♌	+	Fire	Fixed	Sun	☉	Gold	Ruby	Aquarius
6	Virgo	Maiden	♍	–	Earth	Mutable	Mercury	☿	Mercury	Sardonyx	Pisces
7	Libra	Scales	♎	+	Air	Cardinal	Venus	♀	Copper	Sapphire	Aries
8	Scorpio	Scorpion	♏	–	Water	Fixed	Pluto	♇	Plutonium	Jasper	Taurus
9	Sagittarius	Archer	♐	+	Fire	Mutable	Jupiter	♃	Tin	Topaz	Gemini
10	Capricorn	Goat	♑	–	Earth	Cardinal	Saturn	♄	Lead	Black Onyx	Cancer
11	Aquarius	Waterbearer	♒	+	Air	Fixed	Uranus	♅	Uranium	Amethyst	Leo
12	Pisces	Fishes	♓	–	Water	Mutable	Neptune	♆	Tin	Moonstone	Virgo

THE ZODIAC, PLANETS AND CORRESPONDENCES

In the first column of the table of correspondence, I list the signs of the Zodiac as they order themselves around their circle; starting with Aries and finishing with Pisces. In the last column, I list the signs as they will appear as opposites to those in the first column. For example, the sign which will be positioned opposite Aries, in a circular chart will be Libra.

Each sign of the Zodiac is either positive or negative. This by no means suggests that they are either 'good' or 'bad', but that they are either extrovert, outgoing, masculine signs (positive), or introspective, receptive, feminine signs (negative).

Each sign of the Zodiac will belong to one of the four Elements: Fire, Air, Earth or Water. Fire signs are creative and enthusiastic; Air signs are mentally active and thoughtful; Earth signs are constructive and practical; Water signs are emotional and have strong feelings.

Each sign of the Zodiac also belongs to one of the Qualities: Cardinal, Fixed or Mutable. Cardinal signs are initiators and pioneers; Fixed signs are consistent and inflexible; Mutable signs are educators and live to serve.

So, each sign will be either positive or negative, and will belong to one of the Elements and to one of the Qualities. You can see from the table, for example, that Aries is a positive, Cardinal, Fire sign.

The table also shows which planets rule each sign. For example, Mars is the ruling planet of Aries. Each planet represents a particular facet of personality - Mars represents physical energy and drive - and the sign which it rules is the one with which it has most in common,

The table also shows which metals and gem stones are associated with, or correspond with the signs of the Zodiac. Again, the correspondence is made when a metal or stone possesses properties that are held in common with a particular sign of the Zodiac. This system of correspondences can be extended to encompass any group, whether animal, vegetable or mineral - as well as people! For example, each sign of the Zodiac is associated with particular flowers and herbs, with particular animals, with particular towns and countries, and so on.

It is an interesting exercise when learning about astrology, to guess which sign of the Zodiac rules a particular thing, by trying to match its qualities with the appropriate sign.

The News of the Future

In the Almanack

Racing Tips — All the Classics. Dozens and dozens of lucky dates to follow — for Trainers and Jockeys.

Football and Greyhounds too.

Gardening Guide — Better Everything. Bigger; better; more colour. Whatever you want! Lunar planting is the key.

Fish Attack — Anglers get the upper hand and catch more fish. Dates, times and species to fish are all here.

With Key Zodiac Sign dates of course.

A great New Year investment for you.
An inexpensive, fun gift for your friends.

Look for it at W. H. Smith, John Menzies, Martins and all good newsagents.